Pelican Books
Violence for Equality

Ted Honderich is Reader in Philosophy at University College, London, and has been visiting professor at Yale University and the Graduate Center of the City University of New York. He has written *Punishment: The Supposed Justifications* (Penguin) and *Three Essays on Political Violence*, and is a contributor to philosophical journals and other publications. He is the editor of the books *Essays on Freedom of Action*, *Social Ends and Political Means* and (with M. Burnyeat) the companion volumes *Philosophy As It Is* (Penguin) and *Philosophy Through Its Past*, and the general editor of the continuing series of books *The International Library of Philosophy and Scientific Method* and *The Arguments of the Philosophers*.

VIOLENCE FOR EQUALITY

Inquiries in Political Philosophy

Incorporating *Three Essays on Political Violence*

Ted Honderich

POLITICAL OBLIGATION

~~polit~~ obligation to a govt because it pursue moral ends

(i) oblig to obey when you think its policies moral

(ii) oblig to obey when you think its policies immoral, but not dangerously so (because it is a legit govt – ie on whole pursues moral ends)

(iii) NO oblig to obey when you think its policies are totally immoral.

Penguin Books

Penguin Books Ltd, Harmondsworth,
Middlesex, England
Penguin Books, 625 Madison Avenue,
New York, New York 10022, U.S.A.
Penguin Books Australia Ltd, Ringwood,
Victoria, Australia
Penguin Books Canada Ltd, 2801 John Street,
Markham, Ontario, Canada L3R 1B4
Penguin Books (N.Z.) Ltd, 182–190 Wairau Road,
Auckland 10, New Zealand

The first, third and fourth essays in this collection were first published in the U.S.A. as *Political Violence* by Cornell University Press 1976
First published in Great Britain as *Three Essays on Political Violence* by Basil Blackwell 1977

This extensively revised and expanded edition
first published in Pelican Books 1980

Made and printed in Great Britain by
Richard Clay (The Chaucer Press) Ltd, Bungay, Suffolk
Set in Linotype Plantin

[Note – Honderich's "Principle of Equality" is simply a statement of Rawls's Difference Principle in slightly different linguistic form to tone down Rawls' implicit stress on incentives. So Honderich substitutes for Rawls three principles just his last – and lexically last – one.]

To Ruth and Bee

1. What is the just society? (state?)
2. What ought I to do in an unjust society? (state?)

"WELL BEING FOR ALL PERSONS WITHOUT EXCEPTION" (p 173)

CONTENTS

INTRODUCTION

These five essays are what has come of my trying to inquire with an open mind into the morality of political violence, or really, political violence of the Left. To inquire, to try to get away from preconception and the like, this was my explicit intention, and indeed I have found my way to some propositions which are uncongenial to me. This is true of one of several main propositions. Still, I have done rather better at finding congenial ones. Perhaps this helps to show that to open one's mind is not necessarily to lose one's convictions.

It is sometimes said, still, that no question of moral justification arises about violence. It is not that the answer is obviously this, or obviously that, but that the question does not come up. There can be no question of right or wrong since, to speak plainly, violence is not really or finally a matter of the choice or decision of individuals. It is one more part of history's inevitable course. This doctrine of historical inevitability is attributed to Marx, and still labours under the name of Dialectical Materialism. It has had, and will continue to have, some moral and political importance. I do not take it to be clear, or near to being settled as true, or indeed a doctrine which if true would make moral inquiry irrelevant. The last of those three suppositions would be the hardest to prove, but far from impossible.

The members of a second party of amoralists about violence do allow that the question of morality arises but do not allow it importance. They regard it, in fact, as trivial. They are often enabled to do this by a misunderstanding, sometimes a misunderstanding of a wilful kind. That is, the question of the morality of violence is taken to be somehow peculiar to clergymen, muddled dons, risen journalists and other apologists. It is taken to be the question of how violence is regarded by the morally conventional, or by the morally naïve, or by those who are blinded by class prejudice. To put this last possibility differently, the inquiry into the rightness or wrongness of violence is taken to be an inquiry directed by self-serving, rotten moral principles. Such an inquiry is by definition worthless, and I trust, unremarkably, that mine is not of the kind. It would take a great deal of argument to establish that *any* inquiry into the rightness or wrongness of violence, or any but a single chosen one, must of necessity be of the given low kind, or, to return to the other possibilities, a matter of mere conventionality or *naïveté*. Attempts have been made, in fact, to supply the argument for these or related conclusions. It would be unfair to suggest that they have always derived from what I have called misunderstanding.

There is a third and related group of amoralists. Its members do recognize that there is a question of the moral justification of violence, and they do not dismiss or diminish it in any of the ways just mentioned. That is not to say that they do not diminish it, however. They add something which they take to overwhelm it. There is said to be a second question of justification, which is not one of moral justification. There is thought to be no doubt whatever that if violence is justified in this second way, that fact overwhelms its being morally justified or its being morally unjustified.

What is this other warrant that violence may have? In answer the phrase 'the justification of history' may be heard, and such terms as 'social function' and 'historical meaning' and 'meaning for history'. We are to understand, perhaps, that present violence may be justified in the sense that at some future time it will come to be seen clearly that it did in fact make a necessary contribution to the achievement of some millennium. It had the future in it, a large future. Sometimes it is allowed and sometimes it is denied that we can somehow discern, in the present, that something is justified in this sense.

The confusion is plain. What we are told, at bottom, is that violence may or may not make an essential contribution to a great good that is possible. The question of whether it will do so, therefore, far from being something separate, is a part of the question of moral justification. The question of whether violence will make a certain contribution to a millennium is not an independent and higher question, but something which must enter into the inquiry into the rightness or wrongness of violence. It enters in, of course, whether or not it can be answered now.

I mention these three related groups of amoralists, of disparagers of our question, not because I mean to try to deal in any sufficient way with any of their various doctrines. My purpose is mainly to set them aside, some of them as friends misled, and hence to make clear at this early moment my own inclination. It is an orthodox one, that political violence does raise a question of moral justification, and that it raises that question above all.

All of the essays are exercises in political philosophy, or anyway attempts at it, political philosophy being none of political theory, political sociology or, of course, Reflections on the Danger to the Liberal Society. Rather, political philosophy is what results from a different kind of concern for clarity and for orderly reflection and argument. The second and fifth essays, 'Our Omissions and Their Violence' and 'Four Conclusions about Political Violence of the Left', were not in my *Three Essays on Political Violence* (Blackwell, 1977) published in the United States as *Political Violence*. The first, third and fourth essays, which made up that book, have been revised.

The first essay, 'On Inequality and Violence, and Differences We Make between Them', is unlike others in not dealing with the question of the morality of violence entirely by way of argument and reflection of a philosophical kind. That is, it is partly empirical. The facts which are brought to political philosophy, and I trust to its improvement, concern average lifetimes of certain groups and classes. For the rest, the particular subject of the first essay is certain of our first responses to the facts of inequality and the facts of violence, responses both in feeling and in doctrine. The essay is drawn from a lecture given to the Royal Institute of Philosophy.

The second essay, 'Our Omissions and Their Violence', begins from what is said by the violent, or some of them, against those of us who are law-abiding. It is that despite our moral confidence we contribute in an essential way, by our omissions, to denials of life and to misery and injustice. The essay has to do with the reply that there is a great difference between acts and omissions, whatever else is to be said. It has to do, too, with another reply to the violent. I mean the inevitable refrain about any *tu quoque*, that the guilty are trying to avoid the subject of their guilt. Those who kill and wreck are merely attempting an evasion. 'Our Omissions and Their Violence' comes from a lecture first given to a conference at the University of Calgary.

Several pieces of reasoning by others are examined in the third essay and perhaps handled too roughly. One has to do first with the obligation to obey the law and to abstain from violence, and also with what is taken to be a conflicting and a higher demand, essentially a demand of conscience. It is the work of Robert Paul Wolff. The other argument examined in the essay is founded on the idea of a social contract, and issues in particular propositions about the obligation to obey the law and to abstain from violence. It also issues in two principles of justice for judging obligation, violence and much else. It is the work of John Rawls. This third essay is drawn partly from a lecture given to the Oberlin Philosophy Colloquium and partly from a paper contributed to the journal *Mind*.

'On Democratic Violence', the fourth essay, concerns democracy and violence. It sets out answers to the questions of how violence stands to the practice and to the rules of democracy, and, more importantly, an answer to the question of how violence stands to the ends or values which are proposed in the fundamental arguments for democracy. There is, as a result, analysis of a particular kind of violence, named the democratic kind. The essay comes from a lecture to the Third International Conference on the History of Ideas.

What can be saved of the traditional Social Contract argument is a part of the subject of 'Four Conclusions about Political Violence of the Left'. Another part is the consequences of an admirable moralism, an affirmation of moral necessities. Reflection on these two things leads to a further consideration of the empirical issues of inequality raised in the first essay. These in turn lead to principal questions about violence of the Left, and responses to them. The essay comes from a speech to a United Nations conference.

The responses just mentioned, as I say after making them, give rise to an idea which also has a place in this introduction, and needs to be brought into consistency with the idea at its beginning. If political philosophy should be an attempt to inquire with an open mind, it is also something else. It is *advocacy*, in a way related to the work of a decent barrister. Political philosophers are more like barristers than judges, even if barristers more or less convinced of the rightness of their cases, and it is worth remembering.

I am grateful for comments on particular arguments and claims to three of my colleagues, Myles Burnyeat, Jerry Cohen and Malcolm Budd; to Brian Barry, George Brennan, David Hamlyn, Alastair Hannay, Mihailo Markovic, Helen Marshall, Janet Richards, Adam Schaff and Allen Wood; to graduate students who attended a term's seminar on Rawls's book at University College London; and to critics in many university audiences.

I thank Katherine Backhouse, Dinah Perry and Christine Jones for exemplary work in the preparation of the manuscript.

*　*　*

By way of fuller bibliographical detail, the first, third and fourth essays were published as *Three Essays on Political Violence* (Blackwell, Oxford, 1977) and as *Political Violence* (Cornell University Press, Ithaca, 1976).

The first essay is also published in *Nature and Conduct: Royal Institute of Philosophy Lectures* (Macmillan, 1975), edited by Richard Peters.

The second essay comes from 'Clean Hands', a lecture to the Workshop on Justice at the University of Calgary in 1977.

The Oberlin lecture, from which much of the third essay comes, is published as 'Appraisals of Political Violence', in *Issues in Law and Morality, Proceedings of the 1971 Oberlin Colloquium in Philosophy* (The Press of Case Western Reserve University, Cleveland and London, 1973), edited by Norman S. Care and Thomas Trelogan. *Issues in Law and Morality*, incidentally, also contains a reply to the lecture, by Edmund L. Pincoffs, and my rejoinder. The journal article from which the third essay also derives is 'The Use of the Basic Proposition of a Theory of Justice' (*Mind*, 1975).

A considerably shortened version of 'On Democratic Violence' appears in *Violence and Aggression*, Proceedings of the Third International Conference of the International Society for the History of Ideas (Rutgers University Press, New Brunswick, 1974), edited by Philip P. Weiner and John Fisher. The essay also appears in the journal *Philosophy and Public Affairs* (Vol. 2, No. 2, 1973).

The final essay, 'Four Conclusions about Political Violence of the Left', comes from a speech to a UNESCO conference on 'The Rights and Duties Deriving, for States and Groups, from the Establishment of a New International Economic and Cultural Order', Paris, 1978.

I am grateful to the various publishers for permissions.

1 ON INEQUALITY AND VIOLENCE, AND DIFFERENCES WE MAKE BETWEEN THEM

Just about all political philosophy of the recommending kind is fact-less and presumptuous. It is of use in deciding how life ought to be, and how to get it that way, but that it is of use is only to be explained by the want of something better.

We can agree that all of philosophy, in order to come within sight of its several ends, must have far less to do with empirical fact than those disciplines which have the discovery of it and its explanation as their only end. However, in the political philosophy which implicitly or explicitly recommends action to us, or more likely inaction, premises of empirical fact necessarily have a larger importance than elsewhere in philosophy. It is not to be overlooked that recommendations of a quite specific nature are made. We are in fact urged to take a political side.

Political philosophy of this kind, to its lesser credit, is different even from moral philosophy of the traditional kind. There, one is urged towards such traditions as the Utilitarian and such commitments as to integrity. Neither the Principle of Utility by itself, nor a principle of integrity, is presumed to settle particular questions in private morality for one. It is understood that to settle questions of conduct in marriage, say, one needs something in addition to general principles, which by themselves do not tell one what to do. The additional factual premises are not and could not easily be supplied, and so, very reasonably, recommendations of a specific nature are not made. One is not told what to do in marriage.

In political philosophy of the recommending kind, one is told what to do in politics. For such recommendations to rise to being *argued* recommendations, they clearly need to be preceded by premises about society, empirical premises of a quite particular kind about conditions of life. Typically they are not. Nor does one have much confidence that what is said for our guidance was in fact derived, in private reflection off the page, from factual premises worth the name.

If political philosophy of the kind in question, just about all of it, is as little empirical as the rest of philosophy, and has such need to be more so that it may with justice be called factless, it is therefore presumptuous in its conclusions. However, there is also presumption in it for an entirely different reason.

The issue of political violence, to come down to that, is typically handled in a mere essay or a mere chapter, which thing does nonetheless end with a conclusion on the principal question. We may be told that violence, leaving aside a few chosen revolutions now dignified or indeed hallowed by time, is savage iniquity. We may be given to understand, differently, perhaps in something that falls short of plain speech, that violence of the Left must reluctantly be welcomed. It may be allowed, as certainly it should be, that what has actually been set out in support of the chosen conclusion is no more than a *simulacrum* of the argument for it, or, certainly better, only *one part* of that argument. Still, we are offered the intimation that all of the real thing, the conclusive argument itself, exists somewhere else.

This political philosophy, then, begins without essential premises of fact, proceeds by way of intimation, and delivers conclusions to us nonetheless. Let us make a beginning at trying to put things right.

1. Lifetimes

In the United States, on average, non-whites live for about 6·5 years less than whites.[1] About 25 *million* individuals now alive will have an average of about 6·5 years less of life than, on average, other members of their society. The average is produced, of course, by more deaths of babies, of children, of young people, and of their elders. Fewer make it through each stage of life. If there are no very fundamental economic and social changes in America, it is likely that the next 'generation', the non-whites who are alive twenty years from now, will have an improved life-expectancy but still one that is very considerably smaller than that of their white contemporaries. The rate of improvement in the past gives one of several bases for this guess about the future.[2] A more precise guess is that non-whites alive twenty years from now, if fundamental economic and social changes do not come about, will have an average lifetime about five years smaller than their white contemporaries.

The population of England and Wales has been divided into five of what are called social classes. They might also be called occupational groups, since they are in fact defined by the occupations of their members. They are labelled Professional, Intermediate, Skilled, Partly Skilled and Unskilled.[3] The average lifetimes of males in the fifth social class is about six years less than the average lifetime of males in the first social class. (The figure on one calculation is 5·12 years, on a second calculation 5·89 years, and on a third calculation, which seems most realistic, it is 7·17 years.[4]) There are about 1½ million individuals in question. One can guess that in twenty years' time, if fundamental social and economic changes are not made in Britain, the unskilled class (or an analogue) will be in an improved position but still have a life-expectancy very considerably smaller than that of a professional class. More deaths at each stage of life.

Let us have before us, beside the truths and suppositions about individual lifetimes in contemporary America and Britain, two uncontentious generalizations about all Western economically developed societies. We can proceed towards these by remembering that non-whites in America and unskilled workers in Britain have greatly less material wealth and income than other groups in their societies.[5] There are, of course, some non-whites who are better off than some whites, and some unskilled workers who are better off than some members of some other occupational groups. On the whole, nonetheless, non-whites in America and unskilled workers and their families in Britain each are large parts of a poorest group in each of the two societies. We have, then, a correlation between an economic fact and a fact about lifetimes. It is unsurprising. Indeed, the fact that the people in question come at the bottom of scales of wealth and income is the principal part of the complex cause of their shorter lives. This consideration, and many related truths about groups in the other economically developed societies, give rise to the two generalizations I have in mind about all such societies.

The first one has to do with roughly the one tenth of the present population of each economically developed society that has less wealth and income than any other tenth in that society. The generalization is that the worst-off tenth now living in each one of the developed societies will have considerably shorter lives than the individuals in the best-off tenth. It is as good as certain that they will live less long, on average, by five years or more. We must wait for precision until the time, if ever it comes, when more statistical work is done. The second generalization, as may be anticipated, is that if there are not fundamental social and economic changes in the societies in question, the situation will be better in twenty years but not greatly better.

As in the case of what was said of America and Britain, the numbers of people involved is of an obvious importance. There are now, in all of the bottom tenths of the economically developed societies, something like *65 million* individuals.

To turn to a related subject-matter, the table below[6] gives a few specimen life-expectancies at birth for males and females, first for economically less-developed societies and then for developed societies. Males born in Gabon have an average lifetime of twenty-five years. Males born in Britain, taking all social classes together, have an average lifetime of sixty-nine years, which approaches being three times as long. On *average*, males in Gabon die well before what is regarded as middle age in Britain.

LIFE-EXPECTANCY AT BIRTH

	Gabon	*Guinea*	*Nigeria*	*India*	*Colombia*
Male	25	26	37	42	44
Female	45	28	37	41	46

LIFE-EXPECTANCY AT BIRTH

	France	*West Germany*	*America*	*England & Wales*
Male	69	67	67	69
Female	76	73	75	75

The average lifetime of males and females taken together in all the less-developed societies, by one common definition of the latter, is about forty-two years. The average lifetime of males and females together in developed countries, again with the latter defined in one common way, is about seventy-one.[7] About *half the world's population*, then, have average lifetimes about twenty-nine years shorter than another quarter of the world's population. It is not too much to say that what we have before us are *different kinds* of human lifetime.

The average figures for the two groups of societies, as the specimen figures indicate, hide still greater inequalities, those holding between particular poor and particular rich societies. There is also the greater difference in lifetimes between the top tenth of population in all the developed countries and the bottom tenth of population in the less-developed countries. There are no figures available, to my knowledge, for the latter tenth. Given evidence of various kinds, it is certain that the bottom tenth in less-developed societies have average lifetimes very much more than twenty-nine years shorter than the average lifetimes of the top tenth in developed societies. Their lives, on average, are in the neighbourhood of forty years shorter. It is not too much to say, then, that the wealthiest in the wealthy countries have two lives for each single life of the poor in the poorest countries. It is not too much to say that if one knew only the average lifetimes of these two groups of beings, one would suppose they were *different species*.

There is a likelihood that these inequalities in life-expectancy between developed and less-developed societies, and groups within them, will be smaller in twenty years. In the recent past, medical advances have improved life-expectancies in the less-developed societies, and it is likely that further advances will be made. Nonetheless, unless there is a transformation in the relations between the wealthy and the poor parts of the world, there will remain an immense difference in lifetimes twenty years from now.

The numbers of people involved in these propositions about the less-developed societies are of course very great. The population of the less-developed societies, as defined, about half of the world's population, includes about *1,700 million people*. The bottom tenth then includes about *170 million people*.

There arises the question of the possibility of any real change, either in the inequalities of lifetime within developed societies or in the inequalities of lifetime between developed and less-developed societies. Some will be inclined to suppose that whatever morality may say or not say, we do not have the relevant capability. Thus there is misconception in talk of large changes in lifetimes that might follow on fundamental social and economic changes. It may be objected, in effect, that it is already inevitable that the next generation of the groups in question will have a life-expectancy much like that of the present generation of the same groups.

This is mistaken, certainly or probably. Given the wealth and efficiency of the developed societies, proved in many different ways, it is clear enough that we could change very radically the life-expectancy of the groups in question. One needs to reflect, in part, on the magnitude of just such changes in the past. To consider the inequalities *within* developed societies, the following table gives the change in life-expectancy of American whites, at birth, over a period of forty years.[8]

1920	54·9
1940	64·2
1960	70·6

One fact of relevance, then, is that in each of two twenty-year periods in the recent past, the life-expectancy of American whites was improved to a considerably greater extent than would be required in the coming twenty years if American blacks were to come up to the level of American whites.

It is to be admitted, certainly, that the case is not clear with respect to the possibility of change in the lifetime-inequalities between developed and less-developed societies. Nonetheless, it is beyond question that the inequalities could be dramatically reduced. The lifetime-inequalities are consequences of economic inequalities. It is my own view that no amount of economic theory can put in doubt the truth that the present economic inequalities are open to change, change which would not be damaging to present economic totals and which would dramatically reduce lifetime-inequalities.

It is worth remarking in this connection, to those who are struck by how very little *has* been achieved, that not much more than nothing has been attempted. In 1964 a number of the economically developed countries pledged to 'contribute' a percentage of their future gross national products to the less-developed countries. This 'contribution' was to include loans and private investment. The figure agreed upon was 1 per cent. Since that time, a number of the countries in question have failed to reach this percentage. None has exceeded it by much. The pledged total of 1 per cent of the gross national products of the developed countries in question has not been met in any year.[9] This is not the *kind* of thing to be kept in mind in considering the question of capability. A better thing is the 'war efforts' of the past.

All of these generalizations about lifetimes have *all* of their importance in the fact that they have to do with *individual human experience*. It is a banal truth that typically we escape this proposition, or give it the attention of a moment. It is necessary to come closer to the reality of experience. We may do so through one woman's recorded recollection of her daughter.

She was doing fine, real fine. I thought she was going to be fine, too. I did. There wasn't a thing wrong with her, and suddenly she was in real trouble, bad trouble, yes sir, she was. She started coughing, like her throat was hurting, and I thought she must be catching a cold or something. I thought I'd better go get her some water, but it wasn't easy, because there were the other kids, and it's far away to go. So I sent my husband when he came home, and I tried to hold her, and I sang and sang, and it helped. But she got real hot, and she was sleepy all right, but I knew it wasn't good, no sir. I'd rather hear her cry, that's what I kept saying. My boy, he knew it too. He said, 'Ma, she's real quiet, isn't she?' Then I started praying, and I thought maybe it'll go the way it came, real fast, and by morning there won't be anything but Rachel feeling a little tired, that's all. We got the water to her, and I tried to get her to take something, a little cereal, like she was doing all along. I didn't have any more milk – maybe that's how it started. And I had a can of tomato juice, that we had in case of real trouble, and I opened it and tried to get it down her. But she'd throw it all back at me, and I gave up, to tell the truth. I figured it was best to let her rest, and then she could fight back with all the strength she had, and as I said, maybe by the morning she'd be the winner, and then I could go get a bottle of milk from my boss man and we could really care for her real good, until she'd be back to her self again. But it got worse, I guess, and by morning she was so bad there was nothing she'd take, and hot all over, she was hot all over. And then she went, all of a sudden. There was no more breathing, and it must have been around noon by the light.[10]

To my mind, no breath of apology is owed to those who may say that they do not expect to find emotional matter within serious reflection. On the contrary, one must feel remiss for offering so small a reminder of human experience, or feel a despondency in the realization that so little will be tolerated.

2. Violence

The facts of violence are not so much in need of being brought forward. It is a part of what I shall discuss in this essay that we have an immediate and a sharp awareness of them. Nonetheless, should anyone persist in regarding the effects of violence as no more than calculable expenses to be paid for the march of history, it will be as well to assert what should need no asserting, that here too we find facts of human experience. Bombs injure, maim and kill. They end or devastate the lives of their first victims and they bring agony or ruin to the lives of their second victims, those who suffer through others being injured, maimed or killed. The effects of explosions are not only those effects which we find detailed in our newspapers. A man who is blinded or a girl who loses a hand lives on, and, for everyone who is killed, there are others who continue to be affected.

If these are the things of importance about political violence, there is need for a general definition. Political violence, roughly defined, is *a considerable or destroying use of force against persons or things, a use of force prohibited by law, directed to a change in the policies, personnel or system of government, and hence also directed to changes in the existence of individuals in the society and perhaps other societies.* There are other definitions of political violence, certainly, including definitions thought to be more enlightened or virtuous, and we shall return to the matter.[11]

It will be as well to have in mind some extent or magnitude of political violence. What I shall have in mind in what follows is roughly the level of violence with which we have become familiar in Britain, America and elsewhere in the world during the past decade. To put the matter differently, if no more precisely, I shall have in mind campaigns of violence but not violence at the level of civil war. Nor, of course, shall we be concerned with war between nations, which does not fall under the definition of political violence.

Finally, by way of preliminaries, it may be worth pointing out that more will be in question than exactly the violence which has been most common during the past decade. There can be violence directed to other ends than those with which we are most familiar. We shall be concerned with political violence generally, which is to say both actual and possible violence.

3. Facts and reasonings

There are the facts of violence, then, and there are what we may call, if we persist in the use of an anodyne label, the facts of inequality. The latter, of which we have considered only one particular set, claim attention not strictly because they consist in *inequalities*: situations such that one group of people has *less* of something than another. It is that some people have *so little,* judged in an absolute rather than a comparative way, and that this has to do with the distribution of things. They are in conditions of deprivation or distress or worse. The circumstance is not an unreal one which can be imagined, where inequality does not matter much because the worst-off are nonetheless splendidly off. Our real circumstance is one in which the facts of inequality include, and might alternatively be described as, the facts of deprivation, distress and suffering. This, further, is principally explained by the larger shares of goods of the better-off.

My intentions in this essay, which have to do with these facts and with the facts of violence, are two in number. One of them is 'unphilosophical' and has already been realized. It was to make a small contribution, the first of two in this book,[12] to a realization of the facts of inequality. Any such realization, of course, must affect one's view of violence.

The particular set of facts noticed, those about inequality in quantity of life, have a natural priority. *Time alive* is not all that matters, but it matters very much indeed. Still, I do not mean to give this set of inequalities a greater importance, or for that matter a lesser importance, than others. The other facts of inequality may be separated into two further sets. There are those many inequalities which have to do with economic and social life. The list begins with inequalities in food, shelter and health. The extent of such inequalities is only barely indicated by the known immense disparities in wealth and income. The third set of inequalities are political in kind, and have to do with certain freedoms and the lack of them. It is here that one finds demands for equality in national self-determination, and demands for equality between peoples in certain large possessions, notably lands to which there are historical rights.

It cannot be that rationality allows us to avoid informing ourselves of these things which are more or less directly relevant to violence. No more is meant than said: that we are obliged in rationality *to inform ourselves*. As I have already implied, a part of this is a decent approach to human experience in its detail. What is needed first is knowledge, knowledge of particulars, which is to be distinguished from responses of feeling to the facts of inequality, and from judgements about them. No one should overlook, for example, that shorter lifetimes are in clear ways within the anticipation of very many of those who have them and also within the experience of others. With respect to the latter point, there is the fact that if she had lived longer, the death of the daughter would not ever have been within the experience of the mother.

If we were better informed of the facts of inequality, we could with propriety pass on to further things. What is customarily done, as I have remarked, is to press on improperly, to conclusions. What we shall do here, less improperly, is to move forward slowly. We shall not come to a conclusion about the rightness, the permissibility, the wrongfulness or the heinousness of political violence. The matters we shall consider, like the facts of inequality and violence, have a natural place near the beginning of an orderly inquiry.

There is a certain welter of propositions, arguments, theories and doctrines which comes in between the factual premises about inequality and violence and any final conclusions about the morality of violence. I mean, in saying that these things come in, that they must be considered. All of them are reasons or reasonings, or else they can be improved into reasons or reasonings. All of them, obviously, must be made decently clear and explicit before their value is judged. In the end, of course, since they point in different directions, some of them must be rejected, or regarded as of lesser weight.

Here are some examples, all of one kind. We may believe that some governments, perhaps democratic ones, have a rightful authority over the members of the societies in question, and hence that the members have an obligation of obedience. We may believe that all members of pretty well any society, simply by living in it, acquire an obligation to keep some or all of its laws. We may have some idealized conception of the society of justice, and suppose that our actual society is within sight of realizing this conception. Very differently, we may have some ordered set of fundamental moral principles, or a belief as to the best or the only acceptable way of drawing moral conclusions, perhaps a way that is thought to guarantee fairness.[13] Differently, we may be committed to a number of propositions, perhaps got by historical inquiry, about the probability that violence will secure or give rise to social change. Differently again, we may suppose that some political violence has important affinities with the practice of democracy.

Whatever their final value, such reasons and reasonings are certainly of relevance to any verdict on violence. I shall consider most of them, and some others, in the essays of this book. Still, these are examples of reasons and reasonings of a kind correctly described as being at a certain distance from the facts, the facts of inequality and of violence. There are things which are closer to the facts and which may be considerably more persuasive for many people, whether or not they should be such. Some of these latter things, indeed, may determine the weight given to the more distant reasons and reasonings. They often have the character of unreflective responses and assumptions, but, as I have said, they can be other than that.

My second intention in this essay is to look at four of them, perhaps the four which are most important. They have to do with feelings about inequality and violence, the existence of moral prohibitions on certain kinds of action, the supposed irrationality of violence, and the very possibility of having satisfactory principles of equality.

4. Circumstances of feeling

If we were to assemble the facts of inequality before ourselves as best we could, as we have not done, what would be our untutored feelings about them? Among the facts would be those at which we have looked, about more deaths at every age. (i) Within economically developed societies a bottom tenth of individuals, about sixty-five million people, have lives at least five years shorter on average than other members of their societies. (ii) About half the world's population, that of the less-developed societies, have average lifetimes about twenty-nine years shorter than another quarter of the world's population. (iii) One can say with reason that the worst-off in the less-developed countries, about 170 million people, have *one* life for the *two* lives of the best-off in the developed countries. Among the facts of inequality before us, as well, would be those of socio-economic and political kinds. Also, for all these general facts, there would be particulars, particulars of human experience.

We are, we may suppose, people who are moved to some decent degree by the situations of others and have only an ordinary amount of prejudice. We are not *possessed* by ideology or doctrine. We may, as people do, incline to certain social and economic beliefs, but these are not so much a part of us that we have no independent attitude to the facts of inequality.

What would be our feelings about them? The question could do with sharper expression, but let us take it as we have it. Our feelings in the imagined state of knowledge would be considerably different from our ordinary responses now, in our actual state of ignorance. They would be stronger. As I have already implied, we feel less than we might about the facts of inequality, much less, simply because we are ignorant of them. That, however, is not my principal point, which may be approached by noticing that our feelings would have a certain *character*. Many of us, faced with the facts of inequality, would be appalled, dismayed, saddened, affected, sympathetic, wearied, bitter or resentful. The character of these feelings is one of passivity or quietness.

Suppose that on another occasion we have assembled before us the facts of violence. Suppose we have before us killing, wounding, kidnapping, such destruction of property as touches closely on the lives of individuals, and also the consequences of these several things. The difference between what we are imagining and what is the case, between our having full knowledge and our having the knowledge we actually have, is far less here than with the inequalities.

Many or all of us would feel horror, shock, repugnance, disgust, rage or vengefulness. The terms 'atrocity' and 'savagery' would very likely have a place in the expression of these emotions. To come to the principal point, these emotions do not have about them the passivity or quietness of the emotions called up by the facts of inequality. They have a different character.

This difference is a fact about the feelings which we would have, given a fuller knowledge of inequality and violence, but obviously there is a related fact about the feelings we actually do have, with the knowledge we actually do have. It has seemed to me right to come to the matter by way of insistence that we be more responsible about informing ourselves. Certainly it is the difference in *informed* feelings, as they might be called, which is most important. In what follows, nonetheless, we shall almost inevitably have in mind our feelings as they are, and this will not be disastrous. It will certainly not be to the advantage of my argument, but rather the reverse.

Feelings about inequality and violence are obviously of great effect on final moral views about violence. Furthermore, it is certainly possible to regard the responses as *reasons*, or to derive reasons from them. That is, it can be argued that we ought to be directed in our judgements by such differences in feeling, that such differences are right determinants of judgement.

The general ideas that we are guided by feeling in morality, and that we ought to be, are somehow true. That is, some understanding of these ideas makes them beyond denial. Obviously, both matters are complex ones. Let us look a bit at the second one, to the effect that we ought to be guided by differences in feeling.

It is clear enough that we must pay attention to what can be called the circumstance of feeling. We must look to the question of how it is that we come to feel as we do. Few people will say, except in heat, or with personal excuse, that we should not inquire into this. Very nearly all recent moral philosophy, in one way or another, gives explicit adherence to a general proposition of this kind about judging feelings, despite the fact that this philosophy has not got down to hard cases and hard details. What I should like to consider is whether our circumstance is such that we can give an unquestioned importance to our feelings about inequality and violence. There are a half-dozen plain propositions which are of relevance, things which go unnoticed but which are there for the eye to see.

One notable difference between our awarenesses of the two orders of fact is that the *agents* of violence are inevitably in the foreground and the agents of inequality are not immediately to be seen. The man who sets a bomb or shoots another man is precisely within our focus. Not so with agents of inequality. We may of course set out to find them. We may attempt some distinction of the kind that has informed whole traditions of political reflection and action, and issued in works with such titles as 'Their Morals and Ours'.[14]

If we attempt to find the greyer agents, we may have some tolerable success. We shall certainly find a class of people who may be said to accede to the system of inequalities, and who could contribute to change if they wanted. It does not stand in the way of this enterprise that their motivations and personalities are not greatly different from those of the victims of inequality. They do not contribute to change and, unlike almost all of the victims of inequality, they could do so. Their simplest contribution would be part of their wealth.

At least three relevant things are true of this class of agents of inequality. One is that very nearly all of us, readers of books, are members of the class. A second is that the class is immense and hence, so to speak, anonymous. Its members are not some few identified individuals. The third is that the relation of these agents to the facts of inequality is quite unlike the relation of the agents of violence to the facts of that order. No one with his own hands sets a fuse which secures an immense loss of living-time for American blacks or a part of the British population. Much of the latter difference, which I shall not pause to detail, remains if we narrow down our conception of the agents of inequality to individuals who actively obstruct change or, differently, individuals who by their own actions do make for the distress of identifiable victims of inequality.

Our feeling about violence, then, has very much to do with its agents, while our feeling about inequality has less or indeed little to do with its agents. The latter is true because the agents of inequality are pretty well out of sight or, if they are in sight, they are ourselves, they are many and impersonal, and they are distant from their work. The character of our feeling about violence, against the character of our feeling about inequality, is in significant part explained by the matter of agents.

However, to move towards the principal point, there is reason for saying that our feelings about inequality and violence are principally relevant insofar as they are feelings about victims rather than agents. That, although we shall in a way come back to the question, will be agreed by almost all who consider inequality and violence, no matter to what conclusion they are inclined. What matters is suffering, distress and deprivation, and not, by itself, what may be regarded as an agent's callous deliberateness in intention.

It is impossible to agree with Kant that a good will, or a bad will, matters far more than its effects on others, that a good will is the only unqualifiedly good thing and a bad will, presumably, the only unqualifiedly bad thing. If we could subtract all bad and terrible intentions *or* all suffering from the world, we would rightly not be in doubt for a moment about which to do.

We thus have a consideration which must lead us in some degree to discount the vehemence, indeed the violence, of our feeling about violence. If that vehemence were more the product of an awareness of victims, and less the product of an awareness of agents, the circumstance would be importantly different.

There is a complication with which we shall be faced. There are those who will urge upon us a persistent Utilitarianism, or one or another doctrine akin to it. They will object that if it is agreed that our concern must principally be with victims, it must also be agreed as a consequence that we must concern ourselves with agents, conceived just as causers of distress, makers of victims. That is, we must look upon agents of violence as we look upon ordinary non-political lawbreakers if we subscribe to the deterrence theory of punishment. Like an ordinary offender, a man who sets a bomb is a man who is likely to act in the same way again and also a man who encourages others to do likewise.

It may thus be suggested, by way of a ramshackle argument, that we should in no way discount our feeling about violence on the ground that it is to some significant degree called up by agents. The argument, in essence, will be that any discounting of feeling leads to inhibition of it, that inhibition will have an effect on what is done to agents, and that if less is done there will be more victims. Of course, the same sort of premises may also be taken to lead in another direction, towards doubt about the validity of our passive or quiet response to the facts of inequality. That is, the premise about the necessary connection of agents and upshots may be thought also to contribute to the conclusion that we should try to have stronger feelings about the agents of inequality, or compensate in our reflection for the weakness of our feelings.

I shall not examine either this retort or the Utilitarian argument about violence. All I wish to notice is another fact about our actual responses to the agents of violence. In those responses we are not in fact persistently Utilitarian, or anything like it. Our responses to the agents of violence, perhaps, are in part 'useful' responses to causes of distress or, in the relevant sense, makers of victims. However, our responses are very much more than that. They are accusatory or vengeful. The machine that maims a worker and the man who maims another man are naturally regarded by us in quite different ways. In the latter case, there is the fact of our beliefs and attitudes having to do with responsibility and culpability of persons. Hence, even should we be inclined to give some attention to the Utilitarian argument about feeling, it would remain the case that our feeling about the facts of violence has much to do with agents regarded as other than past and perhaps future causes of distress. It is not what some would call rational feeling, in the end about victims.

In sum, the different character of our feelings about violence and inequality has in part to do with awareness of some agents and our want of awareness of others. To the extent that the resulting feelings are not related to the matter of prevention, they are not of the first importance. What is of the first importance is victims. We have, then, a reason for questioning a large reliance on the contrast in our feelings about violence and inequality.

A second plain proposition about our different responses to inequality and violence has to do with the *familiarity* of inequality, which is everywhere, and the *unfamiliarity* of violence. The magnitude of the inequalities, and the absolute as against the comparative condition of those who are worst-off, are not things of which we have much grasp. Still, if we were to assemble the facts of inequality, we would not then have a grasp of something new, something with which we had had no previous familiarity. As for violence not being within the experience of most of us, that is no doubt a generality pertaining only to most times and most places. As such, it stands high among useful generalizations in political philosophy.

It is to be remarked, then, that the quiet feelings evoked by inequality are in part to be explained by the relative familiarity of the subject-matter. The feelings evoked by violence are in part to be explained by the relative unfamiliarity of violence. There is support for this in the truism that there is a deadening or quieting of feeling in certain circumstances, usually in war, when violence becomes familiar.

The suggestion that must emerge here is that the moral relevance of feelings is the less if they owe something, perhaps a good deal, to the familiarity or unfamiliarity of their objects. It surely cannot be that the 'natural' death of a child or the murder of a man has a significantly different value in virtue of there being many or few such deaths, many or few murders. One may think of ways in which the proposition might be qualified, but the qualifications are slight ones, of secondary importance. Thus our circumstance in responding to inequality and violence is for a second reason one in which our first feelings are not to be accorded an unquestioned deference.

A third thing to be considered has to do with the common perception of inequality as *entrenched.* Violence is rightly seen differently. Setting a bomb is a human action which like other human actions might not have been performed. The man could have done otherwise. That, however the belief is to be analysed, is our belief. The action is something, too, which quickly raises in the mind the possibility of prevention by others. The inequalities, by contrast, and for good reason, do not have the perceived character of things that easily might not have been, or things that we can briskly set about altering.

The point again is that if our feelings about human experience are in part given their character by a factor external to that experience, such a fact must be paid attention. If the quiet of our feelings about inequality is in part owed to a perception of inequality as settled and resistant, this is a fact to be paid attention. The terribleness of human experience, the terribleness of having a child whose lifetime is five years, remains just that, whatever may be true about persistence and change. If the inequalities were not merely entrenched, but in fact necessary and inevitable, which is different, the situation would be otherwise. That they are in fact necessary and inevitable is a simple error corrected by some reflection on history. It was once thought to be necessary and inevitable that children worked in mines, and the example can be multiplied a thousand times.

It is to be admitted, certainly, that it would be irrational to come to a verdict about political violence without paying careful attention to the probability of its actually achieving ends of social change. That is something of which I shall have more to say. However, it is one thing to take the matter into account, in full consciousness and in the right place, and another thing not to notice its effect, or rather the effect of something less precise, on our feelings about the human experience of inequality.

Fourthly, it is at least arguable that our feelings about inequalities and about violence are influenced by the correct perception of the inequalities as constituting a state of *order*, and violence as constituting a circumstance of *disorder*. Inequality is a product of law, of diverse settled institutions, of custom and indeed of assent. The vast majority of those who are worst-off do not resist, because they cannot. Violence is otherwise. A man shot by a political assassin is one of two figures in a circumstance of a wholly different character, a circumstance of anarchy. No restraint is put on one's feeling about his death by a recognition of it as ordained.

To repeat, if our concern is rightly our feelings *about the experience of others*, it is important to be sure that we take into account precisely these feelings. The present point, then, is that the pain and distress of others should not come upon one, in the first instance, as items of order or of disorder. It may be that they should be so considered, at some later point in reflection. They should not be regarded in this way in the first instance if a primary matter is not to be confused. If, therefore, pain and distress *do* in fact have an effect upon us which is partly a consequence of something that is external to them, we must recognize this fact.

A fifth consideration has to do with the difference, not necessarily a reasonable difference, in our response to being attacked or wounded on the one hand, and, on the other, being distressed or made to suffer for much longer periods but not as a consequence of being attacked, wounded or the like. Before one rests a conclusion quickly on our primitive impulse to choose, say, lasting hunger rather than an injury, it is useful to consider what one would choose for another person, perhaps a person about whom one cares. Would we have our children hungry for life? It is safe to observe that first impulses are not certain to be last judgements. A sixth consideration has to do with the indiscriminateness or the undirectedness of much political violence. One thing to be remarked here is that the particular victims of inequality are not carefully chosen either. However, I shall leave undiscussed these considerations, the fifth and the sixth, and finish here with something else.

Engels, in *Anti-Dühring*, characterizes all of morality as class morality.[15] It is, in his view, an instrument of the ruling class or an instrument of an oppressed but rising class. A somewhat less *simpliste* view is advanced by Marx and Engels in *The German Ideology*.[16] Bentham and Mill also have views which touch on the general matter.[17] One proposition in this area, one which does not presuppose a ruling class's *devising* of morality, is that some moral feeling has some of its genesis in a self-identification which is general among the members of ascendant classes.

The relative quietness of our feelings about inequality, and the violence of our feelings about violence, are related to our own places in the world. You who are reading this essay, in all likelihood, are a beneficiary of the system of inequality and, perhaps more important, have no human connection with the victims of that system. By contrast, in many ordinary situations of life, you discount the feelings and doubt the judgements of individuals who are in certain positions of benefit and relationship analogous to your own.

It is remarkable that such suggestions of the management of feeling or at any rate self-concern are dismissed by those who are familiar with a society some of whose fundamental institutions are constructed so as to defeat such things as self-deceiving responses to groups other than one's own. It will be remarkable, too, if such suggestions of self-deception and the like continue to be dismissed by philosophers. No recent work of moral philosophy lacks a device against self-deceiving self-interest in its recommended system of reflection. In some cases, the device is most of the system.

Some may regard some or all of the foregoing seven reflections on inequality and on violence as ill-judged or tasteless. This may have to do with a failure to recognize that there are *two* orders of fact, each of them compelling, each of them terrible. Not to recognize this is to fail in feeling and judgement. Again, there is an inclination to suppose the question of political violence, like any serious moral question, is one for ourselves as *moral judges.* That is, it is a question for the moral consciousness or the moral self, or perhaps the conscience. It is not one of which we can rightly treat by bringing in empirical psychology, propositions about the causes of feeling. This inclination, to my mind, is not one to be encouraged. The moral consciousness, somehow insulated from our attitudes and situations, is a fiction, and not a good one.

5. Prohibited acts

There are moral philosophers and the like who say, whether or not they would always do as they say, that there are certain kinds of act which are absolutely prohibited. These are acts about which there can never be a moral question, acts which must never be done whatever the circumstances. Those who express this view, which is connected with religious tradition, do not have in mind such 'truisms' as this, that an act is prohibited if *all* that is known of it is that it would cause suffering. They have in mind certain familiar acts, identified in quite different ways. One kind may be the killing of another person, an innocent person.

It is unlikely that many people would hesitate if they were faced with a straight and clear choice between killing a man on the one hand, and, on the other hand, inaction of which they *believed with certainty* that it would give rise to catastrophic consequences, perhaps many deaths. If, as is far from being the case, they were faced with a choice between an act of killing and, on the other hand, inaction taken to involve the *near-certainty* of catastrophic consequences, many would still choose the killing and would defend their choice. Doctrines about absolute moral prohibition have lost any pervasiveness they may once have had.

Nonetheless, there is no doubt that there exists an inclination or perhaps something more than that, a conviction, against certain acts and those who perform them. It is not the claim that there is an *absolute* prohibition, but it is somewhere in the direction of that conclusion. What is in question here, as before, is the idea that an act of killing, say, is somehow wrong in itself, and not that it is wrong because in fact it will be ineffective in securing an end, say social or economic change. There is thought to be a kind of moral constraint upon us which does not have anything to do with the consequences of action or inaction. It is a constraint which has to do with acts *in themselves*, and one which sometimes may rightly be effective in preventing individuals from doing what would have the best consequences.

This is the second of the responses to inequality and political violence which I wish to consider in this essay. It may be an unconsidered reaction to acts of violence and to those who perform them, either when lives are taken or endangered, or in other cases as well. Alternatively, it may be more reflective. In both forms, rightly or wrongly, it has been persuasive with many people.

The kind of inclination or conviction in question may of course arise in cases that do not have to do with political violence. Bernard Williams, in *Utilitarianism: For and Against*, considers the example of a chemist, without a job and hence with his family in difficulty, who is offered work in a laboratory whose research is into chemical and biological warfare.[18] He, unlike his wife, is particularly opposed to such warfare and to the research. However, he understands that if he refuses the job, the research will proceed anyway. More important, he knows that if he refuses the job, it will go to a particular man who is likely to push along the research with greater zeal than he himself would. The chemist nonetheless refuses the job. It is recommended to us that he has done the right thing. The acute and engrossing argument for this recommendation has to do with two things, integrity, as it is called, and responsibility.

In refusing the job, we are told, the chemist's action flowed from deep attitudes which are fundamental to the person he is. He has not acted as a consequence of the attitudes or actions of another, in such a way as to alienate himself from his own actions, and hence in such a way as to diminish or destroy his own integrity, his integrity in the most literal sense. He would have diminished or destroyed his integrity if he had taken the job, as a consequence of the fact that the other chemist would be more diligent in the research. He would, in that case, have been acting as a consequence of the attitudes and actions of the other man.[19]

To pass on to responsibility, the chemist does take the view, understandably enough, that one of the two possible states of affairs would be *better* than the other. The better one, of course, is the one in which he himself does take the job and hence the research goes forward more slowly than it would in the hands of the other man. However, the chemist also takes it that it is not his business to engage in this state of affairs. It is not *his* business to prepare, however less efficiently than someone else might, for chemical and biological warfare. There is a great difference for him between this possible state of affairs and the worse one. Although he himself is involved by his refusal in the coming-about of the worse state of affairs, *the other chemist does the job* and hence 'a vital link in the production of the eventual outcome is provided by *someone else's* doing something'.[20]

It is allowed that in refusing to take the job the first chemist is responsible, in some sense of the word, for the fact that the research will go forward more quickly than it might. However, this will only come about through the other man's actions. The first chemist cannot be said to *make* this happen, and, it is suggested, he rightly does not accept a full responsibility for the outcome.

In all of this we do have an illumination of the common inclination against certain acts. Certainly there is a great deal of difference between the case of the chemist and the case of a man who contemplates an act of political violence. Nonetheless, any considerations which apply to the chemist also apply to the other man. We may have the inclination that he should be such a man as the chemist. He should be of a certain integrity, and he should maintain that integrity by not engaging in violence, even though he believes that the consequences of his engaging in violence will be, or are likely to be, better than the consequences of his not doing so.

The inclination needs examination, and for several reasons it will be best to proceed by way of the given example of the chemist.

There is one preliminary. The inclination to integrity is in conflict with several general attitudes to the effect that we ought always to act in such a way as to produce the best or the least bad state of affairs. One such general attitude is that we ought always to act so as to produce *the greatest total of satisfaction.* The case of the chemist is indeed offered against this proposition, which is the Principle of Utility in one formulation. However, the inclination also comes into play against the attitude, to speak very quickly indeed, that we should always act in such a way as to produce *that state of affairs which most avoids distress or inequality*.

This attitude, which has informed some of my earlier remarks, and of which I shall say more, is the fundamental part of the most common of reflective moralities. It, like Utilitarianism, is 'consequentialist'. It takes into account only what may be called the consequences of action, although other consequences than are considered in Utilitarianism. It conflicts with the inclination having to do with integrity which has been mentioned. Let us have in mind this particular consequentialist attitude. Let us imagine what is certainly reasonable, that the chemist in refusing the job does something which makes distress or inequality more likely. His action conflicts with the particular consequentialist principle, to express it differently, that we should in all things pursue the well-being of everyone without exception.

The main difficulty about the case, it seems to me, is that of actually finding what consideration or principle it is which is supposed to lead us to agree that the chemist's act in refusing the job is right. That consideration or principle is not actually supplied to us. Let us see what, if anything, can be found.

We are told that the chemist preserves his integrity in refusing the job. This may amount to different things. The first of them which must be got out of the way is the *matter of fact* that the chemist, in refusing the job, is acting in accordance with deep attitudes of his own. His action is in no sense in conflict with these attitudes, whatever they are. Hence we say, if obscurely, that there exists a unity or a whole. *He* remains whole. Integrity, in a literal sense, is maintained. In this, however, we have no consideration whatever that might lead us to agree that refusing the job is the right thing to do. It seems obvious enough that there is no connection whatever between the described integrity and right acts. An act of integrity in this sense, given certain imaginable deep attitudes on the part of an agent, will be an act of absolute immorality. Nothing follows about the rightness or wrongness of the act from the fact alone that it is in line with an agent's deep attitudes, which presumably may be of any kind.

To say the chemist preserves his integrity by refusing the job, then, is necessarily to do something other than state a morally irrelevant and somewhat obscure matter of fact. It is to approve of him, to commend him. It may be to approve of him or to commend him because, as we may say, he is *true to himself*. The chemist perseveres in certain deep attitudes. This second speculation about what is said of integrity is of course related to the first, and it faces a similar objection. It is obviously important what the deep attitudes are. Here there is some obscurity, but it may be that the attitudes are to the effect that *he himself, with his own hands, should not carry forward research into chemical and biological war*. He persists in this attitude even when he sees that it issues in making chemical and biological war more likely. This is how the chemist is true to himself.

There are several related things to be said about this second speculation as to the matter of integrity. One is the general one that there seems to be very little relevant connection between a man being commendable in the given way and his act being right. A man, it seems, can be commendable for the reason that he is true to himself no matter what act he performs, so long as he himself is morally committed to it. All that is required is that he sticks to his moral convictions, whatever they are, having to do with a self-picture or not. An appallingly wrong act, perhaps one of pointless torture, does not move a bit in the direction of being right when we learn that the torturer is being true to himself. What changes, perhaps, is our view of him.

There is the possibility of a confusion at this point. Surely, someone may object, we can support a man in his act, to which he is committed, for the reason that things work out better in the end if people are true to themselves. More importantly, we may sometimes even support a man if *we* think his act is somehow wrong. Several questions are raised by this objection, but it would be confusion to think that it is an effective one. The objector asserts the value of our being true to ourselves *in order to object to consequentialism.* However, the objection itself derives from consequentialism. In part it is that the effects, perhaps in terms of distress and inequality, will be better if people are true to themselves. However, what we are trying to find in the case of the chemist is a consideration or a reason of a non-consequentialist kind, a consideration or a reason for doing what is likely *not* to have the best effects.

The second and lesser thing to be said about commending the chemist is to be distinguished from the point just made that *his act* may be wrong even if he is true to some commitment. It is that if we are even to commend *him*, and, more important, if there is to be so much as a *question* of commending him, we must believe that he does really have something that is distinguishable as a *moral* attitude or a *moral* commitment. We cannot commend a man for integrity on the ground that he is, so to speak, true to his selfishness. An absolutely unswerving record of acting in one's own interests does not establish integrity.

What then is the chemist's moral attitude or commitment? As we have noticed already, he does have *an* attitude: he is opposed to carrying forward research into chemical and biological warfare with his own hands, even though the only alternative is *more effective* research by someone else. Is that a moral commitment? It will occur to everyone that the chemist, in leaving the job to the man who will do more effective research, is simply engaged in keeping his own hands clean. Better that someone else should make a larger contribution to a terrible eventuality than that he should make a smaller one. Better that chemical and biological war should be slightly *more* likely than that he himself should have his hands in it. The chemist may be said to be engaged, if one puts the point in Williams's own way, which might be thought to endanger it by overstatement, in 'self-indulgent squeamishness'.[21]

Williams replies that the criticism is not independent of the assertion of a consequentialist morality. If the point were addressed to the chemist, it would necessarily be no more than an invitation to reconsider his decision, and in particular to reconsider it from a consequentialist point of view. The criticism would not consist in an independent argument, which is what is required, but simply a reiteration of the opposed morality.

This reply seems to me partly right and importantly wrong. The criticism is in a certain sense not an argument, but it need not be merely an invitation to reconsider either. It may amount to the suggestion that it is only self-indulgence which can be discovered to explain the chemist's decision. It may amount, again, to a challenge to produce *a moral explanation* or *a moral reason*. We are indeed told that the unpleasant feelings which the chemist would have if he did the job would be 'emotional expressions of a thought that to accept would be wrong'.[22] However, we are not told the thought, or given to understand anything much about its nature.

What we seem to end with, then, if we look to what is said about 'integrity' in order to find a moral consideration or principle of relevance, is something different, the feeling that the imagined chemist would indeed only be engaged in a kind of self-indulgence.

Do we get further on towards finding a consideration or principle if we direct our attention to what is said about responsibility? To recall, it is allowed that the chemist is in some sense responsible for the research going forward more quickly than it might, since that, as he knows, is the upshot of his refusing to do it himself. However, he is said to be less responsible than he would be if he were to do it himself. He is less responsible for the reason that the other man's activity is a vital link.

There is the possibility of having the wrong thing in mind here. Certainly the chemist's responsibility for research done by himself, *and*, as we can say, *freely chosen*, would be greater than his responsibility for the other man's research. What one should have in mind, presumably, is something else: what the chemist's responsibility would be if he himself went ahead with the research for the strong or indeed coercive reason that otherwise the other man would do it more efficiently. If the chemist did *that*, would he have a lesser responsibility than he has when he refuses the job?

In any case it is far from evident that the rightness of actions has to do with responsibility in such a way that the argument about the chemist is at all persuasive. Let us assume it to be a fact that the chemist in refusing the job is less responsible for the research than if he were to do it himself because of the coercive reason. Let us add in, for what it is worth, that in not taking the job he does not *make* the other man's research happen. Do we now have a consideration or a principle which might lead us to agree that he does the right thing in refusing the job?

I cannot see that here, or elsewhere, we find such a thing. It is essential to the argument, of course, that the consideration be produced. It would not be enough to suppose that it can be perceived, but not reported, by someone of especially good moral vision. That would just be resort to mystery.

Finally and differently, notice that any moral consideration having to do with integrity or responsibility, supposing it can be found and got clear, is of fairly small importance. In a second example,[23] which involves a man's straight choice between killing one person and acting in such a way that someone else will kill twenty, it is allowed that the man's integrity and responsibility cannot stand in the way of his taking one life in order to save twenty. Consequences matter more.

In the case of the chemist, by the way, we are likely to attribute more weight to some consideration of integrity than we should. That is, if we feel inclined to side with the chemist in his decision, we may too quickly attribute this inclination to a consideration of integrity. This comes about, I think, because the case as described is indeterminate. Different possibilities are left open. This in fact brings it into line with reality, but, as can be seen on reflection, it also makes it indecisive as a proof or persuasion about integrity.

Very briefly, we have been assuming of the case that what the chemist should do, if he is to choose the particular state of affairs most likely to avoid distress or inequality, is to take the job, knowing he will do it less efficiently. But that is not entirely clear. One rightly takes it, in thinking of the situation, that there is only a probability that there will be a chemical and biological war to which the research will contribute. But *how small* a probability is in question? If we take it, unreflectively, to be *very* small, so that a war is in fact very improbable, then any inclination we have to side with the chemist may perhaps be explained by our consequential attitudes. That is, we may be moved by the consideration, as people generally are, that a possible upshot very unlikely to obtain must count for less than one which is certain or probable. What *is* certain or probable, if the chemist takes the job, is that he will be distressed, that he will not have registered a protest, and so on.[24]

It remains to transfer these conclusions from the example of the chemist, where attention is not likely to be led away from the principal question by passion or aversion, back to the subject of political violence. What I wish to suggest, although I shall return to the subject,[25] is that one response to violence and its agents, a response having to do with something other than consequences of actions, is at least unclear, and certainly not something of large moral importance. Whatever is to be said against violence, there appears to be no large argument to be found in suppositions of the kind we have considered, about integrity and responsibility, and hence about certain moral prohibitions.

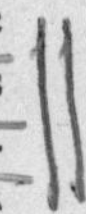

6. Irrationality

Political violence is said to be irrational, and said so often enough that the opinion has a persuasiveness for that fact alone. Let us consider the matter, which is in fact large and ramifying. That it *is* this, rather than something easily manageable, is much of what I wish to maintain.

Some lesser but bedevilling things need to be noticed before we come to what is of most consequence. First, it at least appears that a good deal of slipshod self-persuasion and perhaps persuasion of others goes forward in this area. Let us look at one example. Karl Popper, near the beginning of his essay on 'Utopia and Violence', which has to do with political violence as we have understood it and also with war, writes as follows:

> It ... need not be a vain hope – that violence can be reduced, *and brought under the control of reason.*
>
> This is perhaps why I, like many others, believe in reason; why I

call myself a rationalist. I am a rationalist because I see in the attitude of reasonableness *the only alternative* to violence.[26]

Near the end of the essay, there is this observation:

> Reason ... *is the precise opposite* of an instrument of power and violence...[27]

We are offered an explanation elsewhere in the essay of 'reason' or 'rationality' or 'reasonableness'. It is explained as a certain set of ways of ending disputes, ways which are related at least by the fact that they are all non-violent. They include give-and-take discussion, argument, arbitration, willingness to be convinced, willingness to admit error, and so on.

The sentences quoted may be taken to express sentiments of the right kind. However, they may also be looked at more critically, as indeed they should be. As may be confirmed by reading the essay, they do not have in them propositions which actually are argued for elsewhere. Still, they are not mere bluff declarations that 'reasonableness' is right and violence is wrong. They are more than that, which is not to say that they have argument in them.

(i) In part they are an instance of the simple enterprise of persuasion-by-naming. That is, one set of ways of ending disputes is given a good name or rather three good names. Of course, there is some warrant in ordinary language for using the mentioned terms for the defined ways of ending disputes. There is most warrant for naming them the ways of 'reasonableness'. It is a small fact, and of no use in serious reflection. As we shall see in a moment, it is perfectly possible to describe some violence as 'reasonable', 'rational', or as proceeding from 'reason'.

(ii) In part, the quoted sentences declare a fundamental opposition between violence and 'reasonableness', which opposition invites one towards a general judgement on violence. However, if one is to take the sentences seriously, one needs to know what opposed features of violence and 'reasonableness' are in question, and why these may be thought to make 'reasonableness' invariably right. These questions are not adequately answered, and so we are left without argument. In the place of adequate answers, there is a remarkably unsupported linking of 'reasonableness' with human equality and violence with inequality, and perhaps one other relevant contribution. However, it can stand by itself for consideration.

(iii) That is, one may speculate that the quoted sentences also have in them this piece of persuasion. *'Reasonableness', which is give-and-take discussion and so on, is alone rational, the only choice for a rationalist. Hence it is always superior to violence, which is never rational.* What does the word 'rational' mean here? If we continue to take it to mean something about give-and-take discussion and so on, the proposition that reasonableness is rational is not a premise for the given conclusion or indeed anything much, since it is merely tautological. Give-and-take discussion, etc., is give-and-take discussion, etc. If no different and suitable meaning for 'rational' is given or suggested, we have only rhetoric.

Might the piece of persuasion be turned into something better? Elsewhere in the essay, Popper mentions in passing an entirely familiar and indeed a fundamental conception of rationality. 'An action is rational if it makes the best use of the available means in order to achieve a certain end.'[28] Irrationality thus consists in the adoption of means which do not in fact serve one's end, or serve it at too great a cost. By the use of these conceptions we can certainly escape tautology.

Is it obvious, however, as it should be in the absence of argument, that 'reasonableness' as defined is always or generally rational, the best means to the end? It is not. Is violence the precise opposite, whatever that may be, of rationality in this sense? Is violence never the best means to the end? That is obviously not obvious. As it happens, indeed, it is maintained by Popper in the essay that a good deal of violence is *not* irrational in the given sense, but rational.[29] That is, violence against those who are intolerant or threaten violence is defended as the best means. We thus come to a question about political violence, not a generalization to be used against it.

Before considering this major question, there are three other distractions we may put aside quickly. One, which is also brought to mind by 'Utopia and Violence', is the idea that violence is unreasonable because it is the result of speculation about a utopia, a transformed society. Such speculation is poor stuff, and the activity which follows from it is therefore ill-founded. One thing to be said here is that it is plainly mistaken to suppose that all political violence has to do with the large goal of a transformed society. Most political violence has had smaller ends. It is equally mistaken to run together all reflection which *does* have to do with transformations of society. It is not all of the same quality or kind. For example, not all of it has to do with speculative philosophy of history, as in Hegel and Marx.

The second distracting supposition is that the agents of violence are figures of irrationality in that they are self-deceived. That is, their actions are in fact not done from motives which have to do with the facts of inequality. Their thoughts, and their protestations, are mistaken. What needs to be said about this is that it would be a remarkable fact, one that would distinguish one kind of human endeavour from all others, if those who engage in violence were *never* subject to anything but what they themselves take to be their ends. Equally, it would be remarkable if campaigns of violence with supposed political ends were ever wholly the product, or even in large part the product, of desires unrelated to those ends. It is mistaken to suppose that senseless and unrecognized hostility, and like things, never have anything to do with campaigns of political violence, and it is mistaken to suppose that they often come near to composing them.

The third supposition also has to do with the agents of violence. It is not to be assumed, as often it seems to be, that their own views and defences of their conduct are the only possible views and defences. We do not suppose, generally, that what can be said for or against a line of action is no more than can be said by those persons who are or might be engaged in it. No such requirement survives reflection. No one would deny, certainly, that lines of action and their outcomes are in different ways determined by the beliefs and passions of the agents. Their beliefs and passions, then, must enter into anyone's consideration of the value of their conduct. This granted, it remains mistaken to fix on the agents and to suppose that political violence is to be seen only or precisely as those who are engaged in it see it.

To turn now to the major subject-matter, what may come to mind is something like this question: *Is political violence generally irrational in that it gives rise to distress itself and yet is uncertain to achieve its ends?* It is all right as a question, but only as a culminating, final question. Something like it nonetheless appears to be the *only* question about irrationality which is considered by many philosophers who offer pronouncements. At any rate, they answer only it or something like it. What is certain is that any effective answer to so general and presupposing a question must be supported by explicit answers to quite a number of antecedent questions.

Violence differs considerably in its *first effects* and the same is true of its *aims*. One obvious essential, then, before answering the general question, appears to be a separation of kinds of violence in terms of first effects and aims or ends. Is the kind of political violence which will almost certainly consist only in damage to property, rather than injury or death, a rational means of pursuing equality, or greater equality, in lifetimes and in the quality of life? What of the kind of violence which carries a risk of a relatively small number of injuries or deaths, although it seeks to avoid them, and has the same end? What of the kind of violence, still with the same end, which consists in intentional injury? What of violence, again with the same end, which consists in intentionally causing death?

What of the rationality of violence of each of these kinds but with the different end of *political* equality? What of violence of each of these kinds but with the end not of *achieving* any of the mentioned kinds of equality, but the end of increasing the probability that these ends will be secured in a given time?

There is point in remarking that we can count sixteen questions here, and that more can be added, each of them independent and of importance. Indeed, before considering such additions, each of the sixteen questions needs to be replaced by several which are different in that they contain approximate numbers. Certainly such questions will be regarded as offensive by many, but they are far from unknown elsewhere in human life and they are certainly unavoidable. They are often resisted by those who are worried that they will issue in certain conclusions.

Let us in what follows have in mind but one of them: *Is violence which causes several thousand injuries or deaths, despite attempts to avoid most of them, a rational means of pursuing equalities in lifetime and in quality of life for a society's worst-off tenth, numbering more than five million people?* It will be obvious enough to anyone who hesitates for reflection that we are far from being able to *assume* an answer. This has to do with the fact that the question also raises others.

Let us put aside problems having to do with uncertainty of outcome for a moment. We suppose, that is, that the violence in question would in fact produce the equalities. Would it be worth it? If we are familiar with the existence of such choices, where different kinds of things must be compared, we certainly are not familiar with an effective way of answering them. This is partly a matter of fundamental principles, of which I shall have more to say in the last part of this essay. It is also partly a matter of judging the nature of kinds of human experience. We do not have an effective way of assessing injuries and deaths on the one hand and, on the other hand, the various inequalities and deprivations. We must judge of such matters if we are to arrive at reasoned conclusions about the rationality of violence. Anyone who argues that some violence is rational must obviously deal with comparative questions of this kind. Anyone arguing that political violence is irrational must also do so, although not for so obvious a reason.

To take up what was put aside, the matter of uncertainty of outcome, I have already assumed in these remarks that it may be that some violence is rational even if it is not *certain* to succeed. Although sometimes those who condemn violence seem to suppose that it must always be certain of success in order to be rational, this is a proposition for which argument is needed. There obviously are circumstances in human life where something that is not certain to succeed, or even something that is unlikely to succeed, is rationally attempted. These, of course, are situations of greater or lesser extremity. Very roughly, then, there is the question of how probable it must be that the given violence will be successful if it is to be rational. The answer, which I shall certainly not try to give, will depend in good part on comparisons of the facts of violence and the facts of inequality.

The question will bring to mind yet another, which is prior and as essential. Any view of the rationality of a kind of violence will depend on a factual judgement, or more likely many such judgements, of the actual probability of success, as distinct from the probability necessary for rationality. What is to be said here will have much but not everything to do with the evidence of history. The same applies to the other relevant factual question of probability: How probable is it that given ends of political violence will or would be achieved by non-violent means?

These latter three questions, about uncertainty, are like the others in having presuppositions which must themselves be fixed. What period of time is to be assumed in the last question about achieving ends by non-violent means? That question, if made explicit, must mention a period in which the ends will or would be achieved. The fact of mortality, and hence the length of human lifetimes, suggest a period. I shall not pursue the matter, except to say that it is easier to argue against violence, from a premise about things being better for future generations as a result of non-violent progress, if one's place in a present generation is satisfactory.

Enough has been said to establish that the ready response to political violence which consists in abusing it as irrational is open to question, indeed open to many questions. What has been said, equally, establishes that any unreflective response which consists in the opposite thing, accepting violence as rational, is as jejune. One's conclusion, which there is much point in asserting, must be that the question is an open one.

Such a conclusion is likely to give rise to several different although related responses, which I shall not attempt to discuss adequately. One is that violence must be mistaken in that it causes harm or tragedy and *its rationality has not been shown*. If a general comment is of use here, it is that the choice is not necessarily one between violence, whose rationality is not established, and something else, whose rationality *is* established. There are the same kinds of difficulty to be faced in considering the alternative to violence: non-violent activity which appears to have a lesser chance of securing an acceptable change in the facts of inequality. Perhaps it does not need saying again that a different view, to the effect that this other political activity is already established as rational, is likely to derive in good part from an insufficient appreciation of the facts of inequality. A relevant generalization, obviously, is that situations of extremity do call for the consideration of the rationality of terrible means.

One other thing that may come to mind as a consequence of my conclusion about an open question is that accredited members of societies, as they might be called, are more able to guess what should be done about the facts of inequality. Accredited members include governments and their personnel, leaders of traditional political parties, and so on. Whatever one may think in general of the right of governments to take decisions, it may be supposed that they are in a superior position of knowledge, or of ignorance, when compared to those who contemplate or engage in political violence.

When this is a piece of unexamined piety, as often it is, there is room for that familiar jibe that the wars and catastrophes owed to the accredited members of society do not recommend their judgement. If we depart from piety, and from the jibe, we are bound to find difficulty rather than simplicity. Part of it has to do with the connections between power and judgement, or between power and want of judgement.[30]

My general conclusion here, about which I shall have more to say,[31] is that common responses to political violence, having to do with its supposed irrationality, are themselves unreasonable. In the end, when the work of inquiry and reflection has been done, it may be that the strongest arguments against much or some political violence will indeed be those having to do with the probabilities of success. No doubt we can conclude, now, that such arguments will sometimes be as conclusive as arguments in this area ever can be. No doubt there are situations in which political violence cannot be justified, because it is sufficiently unlikely to work.

It may also become evident in the end, less comfortingly, that violence *would* be justified in these situations if it worked. That is, it may become evident that in these situations, as in others, violence which *did* secure change in inequalities would be preferable to no violence and no change. What may be thought to follow from such a proposition is not our concern now.

7. Principles of equality

Utilitarianism as a basic morality appears to have had its day, and to have remaining to it only a twilight in economic theory. There is no question of our accepting a principle which gives us this general instruction: judge the balance of satisfaction over dissatisfaction to be caused by each possible action or policy, and do the action or adopt the policy which will have the best total, the greatest balance of satisfaction or the least balance of dissatisfaction. Following the instruction may very often satisfy our moral convictions, but we can have no guarantee that we will not sometimes act unfairly or unjustly. Sometimes, if we follow the instruction, we may cause great distress or inequality. It may be that the greatest balance of satisfaction can be secured only by way of the victimizing of minorities or individuals. For example, it may be that the greatest balance of satisfaction in a society will be produced by certain punishments which are certainly intolerable. This will be so, roughly speaking, when the alternative to the given punishments, although it consisted in a loss of satisfaction or even a great total of dissatisfaction, would be so shared out that it was bearable to particular individuals. Utilitarians have of course been aware of such objections to their principle, and have been persistent in attempting to rebut them. They have attempted to show that for one subordinate reason or another, it turns out not to be true that the Principle of Utility does issue in victimization or inequality. In general, their argument has been that if we take into account long-term consequences and various side-effects of possible courses of action, we shall see that the Principle of Utility does not issue in victimization. Their argument, which must go without reconsidering here, is not finally persuasive.

There is then the question of what the alternative basic moral principle is to be. What will come to mind, no doubt, partly as a result of what has been said already, is that we must have a principle of equality or fairness. Certainly the defence of minorities and individuals has always been conducted by way of principles of equality or fairness. What we must also have, in addition to the fundamental principle or principles, although this is not our present concern, are subordinate conceptions, rules and so on. One of these would have to do with forms of government, and others with our obligations to government and with the forms of political activity. Some would pertain to social institutions and others would have to do with private relations between individuals. Such things would be consequences of the fundamental principles.

To announce these needs, however, is to say something less than wonderfully useful. While the conviction that we should have such fundamental principles is not uncommon, we have not got them. They have not been well-defined and rightly elaborated,[32] and so we do not have them in place within our thinking. As a consequence we find ourselves in some confusion about what I have called the facts of inequality. So it is, or should be, with the facts of violence and with any conclusion about its justification.

To provide clear and adequate formulations of the basic principles would be to provide the most important one of the reasonings, as they were called above in the third section of this essay, which stand between premises of fact and substantial conclusions about violence. The full and final devising of the principles cannot be our present business. Let us finish, rather, by reflecting a bit on the difficulty of the enterprise and hence the difficulty of emerging from the mentioned confusion about the facts of inequality and of violence. Are we, as some suppose, in so much or such deep difficulty about principles that a kind of despair is in place, an acceptance of early defeat in our reflections and of what follows from it?

If one picks up a piece of philosophical writing on equality, there is a decent chance that it will describe equalitarian thinking, by which I mean the propounding and defending of principles of equality, as weak, or as incoherent, or as lacking a defensible and substantial principle, or as coming to very little in the end.[33] These claims about the feebleness of equalitarianism, if they are right, show that there is nothing of value to be had from this tradition of feeling and thought. A pastiche derived from these philosophical writings on equality, a decently representative one, goes as follows.

Consider the *Principle of Absolute Equality*, which is that everyone is to be treated absolutely equally in every respect. This is absurd. It is absurd because, for example, not everyone can possibly live by the seaside. Also, we cannot think of treating the sick as we treat the healthy. If more needed to be said of the principle, there is the fact that there is no earthly chance of its being realized, and that if it were realized, the resulting dull uniformity would be appalling.

Let us, then, be guided by the idea just mentioned, that obviously the sick are not to be treated equally with the well. Indeed the only sensible thinking about equality begins from the observable facts that men are different or unequal in some respects and perhaps the same or equal in other respects. The sensible general idea of equality, in fact, is that those who are in fact equal in a certain respect ought to be treated equally, and those who are in fact unequal ought to be treated unequally. This is the *Principle of Formal Equality*.

If it derives from Aristotle, however, it does not carry us at all far. It gives no direction at all until one has found what actual equalities do exist among men. Clearly men are not equal in intelligence, industry and a great deal else. Indeed, it seems that they *are* equal *only* in having certain basic or fundamental needs and desires, and if one can ever get the matter clear, in being *individuals*. That is, perhaps, they are such that they should be treated as ends rather than means.

Given the overwhelming natural differences or inequalities between men, and these few equalities, it is merely confusion to suppose that men ought in *many* respects to be treated equally. Nothing of this kind follows from the Principle of Formal Equality. The most that one can reasonably say is that they ought to be treated equally in such basic ways as these: all should have their fundamental needs and desires satisfied, and none should be deprived of what is called human respect.

We may take this consequence of the second principle and regard it as a principle by itself, that of *Minimal Equality*. It does not require anything like a large redistribution of wealth, or greater participation in social decisions, or an end of social distinctions. It does not require much. What it comes to is something far less than equalitarians have imagined. There is in fact no large and defensible principle of equality.

Equalitarians have also offered many other principles. There is the *Principle of Equal Opportunity* and there is the *Principle of Equality of Wealth*. They have claimed too, if not often, that those who are of *equal merit* should be treated equally, and that those of *equal need* should be treated equally. The latter principle, sometimes expressed as 'to each according to his need', implies the existence of unequal needs, and so is not the Principle of Minimal Equality.

These principles taken together are inconsistent. Equal opportunity issues in inequality of wealth. When these inconsistencies are seen, something must in any case be given up, but how is the Equalitarian to choose? Moreover, it is quite unclear how these latter principles are related to the previous two, those of Formal Equality and Minimal Equality.

If the foregoing sketch were truly a sketch of the best that can be done with notions of equality, we would have some reason for being intellectually dismayed by the prospect of trying to get some moral grip on the state of our societies, on the facts of inequality. However, the situation is otherwise. What follows is only part of what might be said.

Is there really no general and substantial principle of equality, no unqualified ideal which is fundamental to equalitarian feeling, and which would be acceptable as the basis of a basic morality? The first principle mentioned in the sketch, that everyone is to be treated equally in every respect, is certainly unqualified. This, however, the Principle of Absolute Equality, *is* indeed nonsense. It is also nonsense, though, to suggest that it is all that is possible by way of an unqualified ideal.

Notice that it is a principle about *treatment*: that is, roughly, what is to be *done for* and *done to* people. To fix on the idea of treatment is to miss something else that is at the very bottom of ordinary thought about equality. It was presupposed earlier. It is, roughly, the variegated *experience* of individuals, or the qualities of the experience of individuals. These qualities, still to speak generally, come together into satisfaction or distress, well-being or ill-being. There is then the possibility of the principle that everyone should be equal in satisfaction and distress. Things should be so arranged that we approach as close as we can to equality in satisfaction and distress. This is a substantial principle, something with large consequences, but it is unacceptable. We do not want equal distress for everyone if the alternative is good lives for everyone, even if they are unequally good. We do not accept what can be called the *Principle of Any Equality*.

What is required, to put it one way, is that we should improve the lot of those who are badly off, those in distress, even if this does not produce the greatest possible total of satisfaction or the least of distress. This preferable policy will make for a movement towards equality of well-being. This will be so because the level of the hitherto badly off will be raised. Also it *may* be that a necessary means to this end will involve reducing the well-being of the better-off. The principle is against distress and hence any inequality which causes it. We are right to call it, simply, the *Principle of Equality*. Its further formulation and defence lead one to problems, but at bottom it is simple. It lies behind one's being appalled by the great differences in lifetimes with which we began.

This great principle does not carry the inane consequence that we must treat everyone alike, the sick with the well. It is worlds apart from the Principle of Absolute Equality. It does not have the inane consequence since not all people are badly off. Nor, evidently, does it have the sort of practical disability exemplified by the frivolous idea of having everyone at the seaside. It does not even require that all of the badly off be treated in exactly the same way, partly because they are badly off in different ways. For a multitude of reasons, one related to differences between the badly off, there is no danger, if that is what it is, of a dull uniformity. Is the principle open to the objection that there is no possibility of concerted action in accordance with it? It is then like other such principles. It obviously does not follow that it should not direct our efforts. Some argue, with reason, that it is mistaken to recommend a principle which is so utopian as to have no chance of coming to direct the lives of people. The Principle of Equality is not so unworldly as that.

Further objection may be expected from many philosophers. They are those who have assumed, with Aristotle, that all principles of equality necessarily rest on factual or natural equalities and inequalities. They have assumed that one must find an equality of fact, perhaps intelligence, in order to *justify* an equality of treatment.

There is no such general requirement and certainly there is no such requirement on the Principle of Equality. Indeed, to think one is in place appears to require some confusion with an obscure aesthetic principle, having to do with symmetry, or perhaps some speculation that we must act in accordance with the instructions of a god, instructions which he has made implicit in his creation. The Principle of Equality, if anything does, stands as self-recommending in moral thought. It does presuppose certain similar potentialities in all men, which is an entirely different matter from finding a justification in these similarities. It directs our attention not to factual *equalities* but rather to factual *inequalities*. We are not to mimic factual equalities but rather to compensate for factual inequalities.

To return to the sketch, and to the Principle of Formal Equality, it will now be evident that we have no need to search out sufficient factual similarity between men so as to secure the small conclusion that fundamental needs and desires should be satisfied and that persons should be accorded a certain respect. That is, we need not struggle towards, and end with, the Principle of Minimal Equality. We already have a principle which secures the things in question and also a great deal more.

This is not to say that there is no place for anything like the Principle of Formal Equality. Quite the contrary, since the fact of the matter is that without it nothing could count as a morality. Anything which was not in accordance with it could be no more than inconsistency and indeed caprice. Adherence to the Principle of Equality will then involve the Principle of Formal Equality. If two people are badly off in the same way and to the same extent, they are to be treated in the same way. If the Principle of Equality is in accordance with but has no special connection with the Principle of Formal Equality, things are different with the principle or maxim 'To each according to his needs'. This principle or maxim is in fact an expression, indeed the traditional informal expression, of the Principle of Equality. This is so, at any rate, if one understands needs in an ordinary way. The relation of the Principle of Equality to a further maxim, 'From each according to his ability', is not so clear. *How* the badly off are to be helped is not specified by the principle. It does not in itself specify contributions from the more able.

To persist for one more moment with the sketch, it can certainly be allowed that in working out the equalitarian part of a basic morality, or, better, in working towards basic morality by way of equalitarian attitudes, one will certainly have to deal with conflicts between secondary principles of equality. Obviously, the principle of equal opportunity does sometimes conflict with other things. However, it is only if one has a remarkably simple view of human existence, and is forgetful of an immense amount of moral and religious reflection, that it will come as a surprise that principles do conflict, and some must be discarded. It is no cause for despair. What one needs to do is something which is possible, some decision-making, guided by the Principle of Equality.

There would be no point in going only a little way further here with these reflections. I shall have something more to say of basic principles in the third essay. What I wish to suggest here is that in considering the facts of inequality, or, as they might as rightly be called, the facts of distress, we are not at sea. In particular, while it would be footling to suggest that there are no problems, we are not so confused about basic principles as to be unable to make a decent response. It is not that the facts of inequality, or of violence, must defeat moral theory and commit us to a passivity of judgement.

2 OUR OMISSIONS AND THEIR VIOLENCE

Is there not all the distance in the world between our lives and the lives of the violent? Is there not a difference in moral kind between our conduct and theirs? Almost all of us believe something like this. We believe that our ordinary conduct in life is right, or right on the whole, or right enough, and thus far away from the conduct of those who kill, maim and wreck for what they take to be purposes of justice. That is wrong, worse than wrong. The belief that I have in mind is about kinds of conduct, not kinds of people. No doubt almost all of us are also confident that we are better persons, morally better, but what I have in mind is a contrast between acts as distinct from agents. Acts are as related but different subject-matter, as indicated by the simple truths that one can do the right thing for a bad or shameful reason, a reason that lowers or ruins one's standing as a person, perhaps marks one as inhumane, and one can also do the wrong action for a reason or from a feeling that does one credit.

Most of those who engage in political violence of the Left do not agree with our view of their conduct and ours. If we look to what they say in disagreement, what we find may be bound up with a Marxist or another ideology, or with some history of wrongs done to a class or a people or a group of peoples. From each of these things, however, it is usually possible to take away a general proposition that can be considered on its own, free of certain doubtful presuppositions, of obscurities, encumbering terminologies, and too much of the past. It is that we who are law-abiding, contrary to our common belief, do not live lives which are anything like right on the whole. *Our conduct is wrong.*

The argument for this is that by our ordinary lives we contribute to certain terrible circumstances. We make essential contributions to the shortening of the lifetimes of whole peoples and classes, and to many kinds of suffering and distress and degradation, and to denials of autonomy and of freedoms. In fact we *ensure* by our ordinary lives that multitudes of individuals die before time, that families exist in single wretched rooms, and that this or that people are powerless in their homeland, or subservient in it, or driven from it.

Of course the judgement by the violent that our conduct is wrong will be taken as in several ways mistaken, no doubt as absurd. At best, it will be said, it is *tu quoque*, a retort by the guilty that their accusers do wrong. As with *tu quoques* generally, it will get a scornful reply, to the effect that the guilty are trying to divert attention from their conduct, trying to change the subject, perhaps a subject which finally they cannot face. This is too quick. There is a general question about such *tu quoque* retorts and such replies to them. If a *tu quoque* can be established as true, is it nonetheless to be ruled out of bounds? More particularly, if it can be shown that we all do wrong in our ordinary lives, can this be put aside? Can it be shown that *nothing* follows about the conduct of the violent? It may be, rather, that certain things are somehow inseparable, in logic or in fact. I shall now take this to be true, and in the end say more about it.

There is the prior question, certainly, of whether it actually is true that we do wrong in our ordinary lives. Of course there are replies to this. A principal one of them, which is my subject of this essay, is that our ordinary conduct, even if it does contribute to terrible circumstances, consists in no more than *omission*. It is not as if we *acted* to shorten average lifetimes or to secure other terrible ends. That, of course, *would* be wrong. It may be argued in support of this that there is a certain difference of fact between *every* act and the related omission, a general difference of fact which issues in a difference of morality. In virtue of the general difference an omission may be right or at any rate less wrong when a related act would be wrong or more wrong. It may be argued alternatively that there is a limited difference. *Some* omissions, including the ones in question, differ from the related acts in a factual way, with the given difference having similar moral effects, similar effects with respect to the rightness or wrongness of actions.

But (1) is there really a morally important difference of fact between every act and the related omission? (2) Is there a difference of fact between *some* acts and their related omissions, which difference gives rise to a difference in rightness? Rooted beliefs are in question here, but a small number of moral philosophers[1] have nonetheless been inclined to doubt or deny that there is a general difference that will do the required work. Some have also doubted or denied that there is any difference between even some acts and their omissions that makes for a difference in rightness in those cases.

My intentions in this essay are to deal with these two general issues about acts and omissions, and so to arrive at or at any rate come closer to a decision on the judgement of the violent that we in our ordinary lives do wrong. The two mentioned issues about acts and omissions are a subject which is wider than that of political violence, a subject which has not often been discussed in relation to political violence and perhaps never at all in what can be called a non-ideological way. It does not begin to follow, of course, that the issues are not relevant to violence.

It is true that acts and omissions is a subject in itself. To anyone who feels a reluctance to consider one whole subject in the context of another, it may be worth remarking that in political philosophy as elsewhere one can keep one's nose too much to the grindstone. There is a kind of concentration which defeats its own end, or at any rate does not advance its own end, the end of getting a clear view of something or of fixing its true weight. Given our concern with political violence, we might spend time not only on the general question of acts and omissions, but also on war, and on punishment by the state, and on other things. Their relevance to political violence is of several kinds, and it is considerable. If it is true, as it seems to be, that most of the wars of the past ought not to have been fought, and if we were to come to have an understanding of their wrongfulness, we would be more able to judge political violence. So too with punishment by the state, whatever its recommendation or want of recommendation.

1. Six conceivable acts and actual omissions

The conceivable act of sending poisoned food parcels to India is not one that it would cross our minds to perform. However, how is this possible act related to our omitting to give what money we could to Oxfam, or to some other starvation-relief organization? The result of our omission is that some people die.[2]

We would not knowingly vote for a political party which aimed to secure that the economically worst-off tenth of the population in European and other economically developed societies continues to have an average of about five years less time to live, whatever the party had to say about the deserts of these people and their betters. How does the conceivable act of voting for such a heinous party stand to our omission in not really working to try to change these average lifetimes?

We would not contemplate infecting others with serious diseases, but we do not try to secure, as we could, that people have equal and more than minimal medical care. We do not try to secure that end for people in our own societies, let alone people generally.

We would not remove library books from poor schools, whose pupils can have but the smallest hopes in life. Most of us would not try to increase our private profits by evicting families and hence making them homeless. But we do not work as we might for equal and good education, and we do not work for an end to homelessness.

We would not contribute funds to a dictatorship, or to a minority engaged in denying autonomy to a majority. At any rate most of us would not. However, we do in fact fail to contribute funds to political movements against dictatorships, and to political movements against oppressive minorities.

Some may say that there are more 'realistic' ways of dealing with starvation than by contributing to Oxfam, and more realistic ways than those mentioned or implied of dealing with curtailed lives, ill-health and disease, bad education, homelessness and oppression. Suppose that there are better ways, perhaps joining this or that political party or forwarding some sort of economic policy, perhaps one of 'self-help'. This will not matter much to our inquiry.

Just as we do not contribute what money we could to Oxfam, we do not do these other things either, whatever is to be said of their worth. We omit these too, thereby as quickly raising the problem of omission.

2. Comparisons

In what ways are acts and omissions the same and different? Let us consider similarities and differences, differences which hold between all acts and their related omissions and also differences which hold between only some of them.

(i) An act is a bodily movement or stillness deriving from intention, or a sequence of movements or of movements and stillnesses. To say this is to move with some speed past a number of philosophical questions, one of them about the nature of the mentioned connection between intention and movement, the connection described by saying the second *derives* from the first. Still, it surely is no longer the case that the given definition of an act is controversial. Certainly the definition does not make an act into just a movement or stillness. Rather, an act is a movement or stillness with a certain mental ancestry.

What is an omission? One thing to notice is that the term 'omission' can be used in a number of ways. To mention two, it can be used for (a) *the omitted action*, or what was omitted or not done, and also (b) for *the omitting action*, or what was done instead. If I omit to turn off the wireless at 12 noon, we can use the term 'omission' for what I did not do: turn off the wireless at 12 noon. An omission in this sense might be described as an unrealized possibility, or indeed as a mere nothing. Perhaps this conception has had something to do with rather vague scepticism about omissions being morally important. How could a mere nothing be wrong? Of course, this could not be the only conception we have of an omission. Not all omissions could be mere nothings. This is so, to mention but one reason, since we do often *witness* what we call omissions. These, obviously, are omissions in the second sense, exemplified in the example not by *my turning off the wireless at noon* but rather by *my not turning off the wireless at noon*. An omission in the second sense, which is the more important one, and the one with which we shall be concerned, is clearly not an unrealized possibility.

How did I not turn off the wireless at noon? As it happened, I did not turn off the wireless at noon by *staying my hand*, by performing that little action after having made a first move towards turning off the wireless. In staying my hand, further, I did not turn off the wireless. We can correctly say more than that it was *by* staying my hand and *in* staying my hand that I did not turn off the wireless at noon. My staying my hand *was* or *was identical with* my not turning off the wireless at noon. What we come to, then, is the idea that an omission, in the most important sense of the word, is an action, or, as we may add, a sequence of actions. My not going to the West End over the weekend was my staying in Hampstead.

We have not got a difference between all omissions in this sense and their related acts, obviously, but a sameness instead. Omissions like acts are bodily movements or stillnesses deriving from intention, or sequences of such movements and stillnesses. We might well refer to omissions and acts as negative and positive actions. I shall in fact stick to the familiar terms, 'act' and 'omission'. (I shall use the term 'action', by the way, as against 'act', for either an act or an omission.) We shall of course see more of what leads us to regard two actions as being an act and omission, as related in that way. One main thing is that there is the same or a similar or a connected upshot on the whole. Another, is that when either the act or the omission is done, the other was possible.

There is of course a great difference between an act, taken as something actual, and an omission in the sense of *the omitted action*, since the latter is *not* something actual. It is important not to run omissions of the two kinds together. It is possible to do so, and to become a bit mystified, partly because an omission in either sense brings in an omission in the other. If there was an omitted action, there must have been the omitting action, and if there was an omitting action, there was what was not done. It is not necessary, but it will be simplest for us to proceed in terms of omissions in the sense of *omitting actions*. These, to repeat our first proposition, are like acts in being certain bodily movements or stillnesses, or more likely sequences of these.

(ii) Are all omissions simply actions described in a negative way, actions with descriptions which include a 'not' or something like one, while the related acts are described affirmatively? The trouble with this simple idea is that we do not actually get a division into acts and omissions, since each and every action falls under both affirmative and negative descriptions. My not turning off the wireless was also my staying of my hand. Another idea is this one: an omission is an action or a sequence of actions which falls under a negative description *for the agent*, while the related possible act would fall under an affirmative description for the agent. That is, the agent describes the omission negatively and would describe the act affirmatively, whatever other people do or would do. This is so because his intention was what it was. We can imagine a doctor, for example, who carries on in a certain way, which does not include giving penicillin to a badly deformed infant to save him from pneumonia, and describes his action as *not trying to keep the infant alive*. He would describe a related action, perhaps the giving of a lethal injection, as *killing the infant*.

This common idea is no better at giving us a general distinction between acts and omissions. It does not give us a difference between every act and the related omission. Consider another doctor who also carries on in such a way that a person dies. He too does not give penicillin for pneumonia. However, he describes his behaviour as *letting the person die*, or *freeing an incurable patient from suffering*, or *doing my duty*. One of these affirmative descriptions is chosen by him. He may even refuse, for whatever reason, to describe his behaviour as *not trying to keep the person alive*, and also refuse to use any other negative description. This is certainly possible, however unlikely. The plain fact is that this would not stop us from regarding his action, when compared with giving a lethal injection, as an omission. We here have an omission and a related act such that the omission is not negatively described by the agent.

If we return to the six examples given above, we find the same thing. If we compare sending a poisoned food parcel to India and omitting to contribute to Oxfam, we shall take the first to be an act and the second the omission even if the agent prefers to describe the second act affirmatively, as *buying wine* or *saving money* or *looking after my own children*. This is not to say anything of the rightness or wrongness of the actions, of course. In each of the other five examples, the same is true. No matter the description of the agent, the second act of the pair counts as the omission, for reasons to which we will come.

Still, there is something else to be said here. We all have a *tendency* to describe the acts affirmatively and the omissions negatively. This is the natural thing for both the agents and others, evident enough in what has been said so far in this essay. For what it is worth, then, we here have a difference of fact, our first one, but one between most rather than all acts and omissions.

What is the explanation of this fact that in the case of most acts and omissions, the omissions are described negatively and the acts affirmatively, by both the agent and others? The question is of interest to us for several reasons. It may be suspected that there is some *general* difference of fact concerning acts and omissions which is a part of the explanation of the linguistic tendency, which general difference of fact may give rise to a difference in rightness. (The idea would be that the general difference of fact, for some reason, does not always give rise to negative description of the omission and affirmative description of the act, but it does always affect rightness.) Again, it may be suspected there is a limited difference of fact, concerning *some* acts and omissions, which difference wholly explains our linguistic tendency and gives rise to a difference in rightness in the case of the given acts and omissions.

There is of course an explanation of our linguistic tendency, but, as may be anticipated, it has to do with *us* rather than with acts and omissions in themselves. That is, it does not have to do with any fundamental properties of some actions but not others, which properties are such as to call out for the word 'not' in their description.

Notice first that it does seem to make sense to say that there are differences between things as affirmatively described and things as negatively described. An affirmative description is such that a thing so described *has a property* and a negative description is such that a thing so described *lacks a property*. An affirmative description, secondly, brings in a single property such as redness, while a negative description brings in a collection of properties, those which are other than redness. Whatever may be thought of these claims, which are a part of the traditional philosophical problem of negation, they do not get us the conclusion that it is a difference in fundamental properties of acts and omissions that explains our tendency to describe acts affirmatively and omissions negatively. This is so, to repeat an essential point, because any action which falls under an affirmative description also falls under a negative description. In every case there *are* true affirmative and negative descriptions, whether or not we are inclined to use one sort more than the other. Of every action without exception, then, we can say that it has properties of a kind associated with *both* affirmative and negative description. The explanation of our linguistic tendency does not have to do with there being two separate lots of things, one with one sort of fundamental property only, and the other with the other. All of the things have both sorts.

The true explanation of our linguistic tendency must be otherwise. Let us speculate about what may be part of it. This has to do with an established habit which we carry over from a significantly different kind of situation, but one in which we also talk of what we call omissions. It would in any case have been a good idea to distinguish and set aside this kind of situation and usage. Not to do so would have left open a door to confusion.

In this situation there is no pairing of actions of the kind we have been noticing. To begin with, we speak of an omission but there is no related act: no act with an identical or similar or connected upshot on the whole. On the contrary, there is an opposite upshot. In this kind of situation, secondly, it is more or less generally accepted that the agent had a particular duty to do what he did not do. There is a generally accepted rule, perhaps a law in the ordinary sense. Obviously this is different from the sort of situation and talk which is our main subject-matter. The duty and the rule or law, thirdly, pertain to an individual's special position or rôle. For this reason, by the way, we can call the omissions in question *rôle-omissions*.

Consider a judge, who has a duty to give a certain instruction to a jury, at a fixed point in a trial, so that they will not be prejudiced against the defendant in a certain way. This is specified by law.

Suppose the judge says nothing at the given point. We call this an omission, certainly. However, we do not have in mind a certain conceivable act with an identical, similar or connected upshot on the whole. If we did, it would be more or less this: the act of instructing the jury to *have* or to *act on* a certain prejudice against the defendant. (We in fact have in mind the action of so instructing the jury as to try to *prevent* prejudice.) We think the judge's omission is wrong not because we have compared it with the conceivable act but because the judge went against his duty, fixed by law, in his act of omission.

It is our established habit to describe an omission of this sort, a rôle-omission, in a negative way. This is so, presumably, because there is a settled rule which specifies that a person is to do precisely such-and-such. His error, according to the rule, is most precisely or carefully described as not doing such-and-such, and some care and precision are natural in important and more or less formal circumstances. More might be said. Whatever the reason, however, there is the fact of our established habit with rôle-omissions. To come to the main point, it is fairly certain that it is part of the explanation of our tendency to use negative descriptions for the other omissions, those with acts related to them in the way we know. 'Nots' are standard in connection with rôle-omissions, and so come to be used with the other sort of omissions.

(iii) Is the causal connection between an omission and the result different from the connection that would hold between the conceivable act and the result? It is sometimes supposed that it is very different indeed and significantly so. It has been said that the result, perhaps a harm, would be the result of one's movements in the case of an act, but, in the case of the omission, it is the result of conditions which one omitted to change. These words are not terribly clear, but they manage to suggest that the act would be more efficacious than the omission with respect to the result. An act would somehow be *more of a cause* than the omission. There is the same suggestion in the related statement that the great difference between an act of mine and an omission of mine is that the result of the omission would have occurred even if I had never been born, but that is not true of the act. The same children who are now deprived of good and equal education would also be deprived of it if I had never existed. On the other hand, the result of my conceivable act of removing library books from poor schools would of course depend on my existence.

Certainly there is a truth in this last point, of whatever significance. *One* way in which it can fail to happen that I do something is by way of my not existing at all. It is plainly false, however, that my failing to do something, a particular action, is in any way less efficacious with respect to a result than would be my doing something, another action. The omission is precisely as much of a cause as the act would be. Staying my hand at noon, my not working for good and equal education, each does obviously make a difference. It will be as well, however, to have some details of the causal nature of acts and omissions.

An act in almost every instance would be a necessary condition, in the situation, of a result. That is, the result would not happen in the situation without the act. Also, the act would be part of a causal circumstance, a set of things sufficient to produce the result. That is, it would be part of something which necessitates the result, which would not obtain without being followed by the result. Indeed, the act would *complete* the causal circumstance: the other things would already be on hand. Sending a poisoned food parcel would be a necessary condition, in a certain situation, of certain deaths: the deaths would not happen without the parcel. The act would be a part of a causal circumstance which was sufficient for the deaths. It would complete it.

We can say near enough the same things of an omission of mine, say the action by which I got rid of £500. Suppose I bought a chaise longue. It would be mistaken or misleading to suppose that doing exactly that was a necessary condition of the death of a starving person. Still we can suppose that a necessary condition of the death was that in one way or another I omitted to contribute £500 to Oxfam. By my action I did supply the necessary condition. That fact is not put in question by the fact that I might have supplied it another way. Furthermore, my omission was part of a causal circumstance sufficient for the death. It completed that circumstance. Given all this, it is certainly mistaken to think that the act of sending poisoned food would be more efficacious, more of a cause, than the omission. Similar comments, although not exactly the same ones, are in place with our other five examples of act and omission.

It is clear enough that very often the causal circumstance in connection with omission and result is in another way different from the circumstance in connection with act and result. In the case of the omission, the rest of the causal circumstance for the result is likely to include the omissions of other people, perhaps many other people. Consider the result which is the particular loss which may be said to result from my failing to work for equal and more than minimal medical care. The omissions of many other people are also parts of the causal circumstance for that result. If we turn to the conceivable act, my intentionally infecting people, there is at least the possibility that my act would be the only action in the causal circumstance for the result. Related remarks apply to all but the second of our six examples, the one having to do with voting for the appalling political party.

It would also be misleading to describe this difference in connections by saying the omissions usually are lesser causes than the related acts would be. They have much the same causal features, those enumerated a moment ago. There is only the difference here that it is usually true that actions of others, perhaps many others, enter into the causal circumstance for the result in the case of omissions, and this would not be so in the case of the related acts. There is the related small fact that it is generally true that if I act, intending to cause a harm, there is a small possibility for others to prevent the harm, but if I omit to act, thereby not myself preventing the harm, there is a larger possibility. I leave more scope for good works and self-improvement by others if I omit to act. There is not much to be made of this, of course, unless one brings in certain religious ideas which are now of the past, and which surely were never sufficient to their tasks.

There may also be other differences having to do with causation between acts and omissions. Often but not always the causal chain or causal sequence in the case of acts would be shorter or 'simpler' than in the case of omissions. Clearly enough a causal circumstance is not less efficacious simply because its linkage to the upshot is of either of these kinds. It is true that certain other features sometimes go with shorter as against longer and 'simpler' and as against 'more complex' causal chains, and we shall notice these features in due course.

(iv) If we consider omissions from the point of view of the intentions of the agents, we can make a very rough division into three categories. It has to do, in part, with the fact that any action, as an omission, has what we can call a certain nature or character and a certain effect. One of my omissions is *not contributing money to political movements against dictatorships*. That description gives the nature of the omission. The effect is that the given political movements are to a degree weaker. It is the agent's relation to the character or the effect of his action that determines, as we can say, whether his omission was fully intentional, partly intentional, or unintentional.

Fully intentional omissions are most likely to occur in medical contexts. Consider the doctor who continues his ward-round during a certain time. To do this is to perform a certain omission, failing to give penicillin to a patient for pneumonia. This has as its effect the death of the patient. If the character of his actions or their effect, as we can say, was the intention of the doctor, then the omission was fully intentional. To put it differently, if the actions derived from an intention which the doctor would characterize to himself as the intention not to give penicillin to the patient for pneumonia, or the intention to bring about the death of the patient, then his actions were a fully intentional omission.

It is worth noting that the intentions that issue in fully intentional omissions are in all respects like the intentions that issue in fully intentional acts. Some are *impressive*, as we might say, since they involve internal resolutions or declarations to do such-and-such, and some are not. Some are such as to *take up* or occupy the whole attention of their agents, and some are not. Some are formed under *higher-order* intentions and some are not. Some are, so to speak, something like the whole story of what the agent is thinking and feeling, and some, no doubt most, are not.

Partly intentional omissions are connected with *earlier* actions and their intentions. The earlier intentions are more important than the *immediate* intentions of the omissions, those that just precede or accompany the omissions. Out of bloodymindedness, I do not write down a note of an unpromising engagement when asked. I have it in mind that I may forget. There is the result, given my general forgetfulness, that I do forget and do not turn up. My not turning up is one example of a partly intentional omission. Here is another. I look away from the Oxfam advert in my newspaper, including the photo of the starving child, my intention being not to be troubled or got at by it, and indeed not to have to face a moral challenge and to give money. There is the result of this action and a multitude of related ones, that I later buy wine without thinking that doing so is in fact not contributing to Oxfam. A partly intentional omission, then, does not in fact derive from an immediate intention which specifies its character or effect, for the reason, roughly speaking, that the agent has so acted earlier that it will not. A partly intentional omission does derive in part from an earlier intention which does have in it something of the character or effect of the later action. The earlier intention has something of the later omission in it. Needless to say, the characterization is very vague. Needless to say, as well, there are many sorts and varieties of what have been labelled partly intentional actions. In fact, my main argument has not much need of greater detail, but I shall say a bit more later in other connections.

Unintentional omissions, finally, are those whose characters and effects are not intended by the agent, and it is not the case either that this is so because of earlier activity of his. He did not so act or plan or contrive at an earlier time to have the omission out of mind when he performed it. If the idea of an unintentional omission comes to anyone as a surprise, this may partly be because of the fact that there is a tendency to think of all 'omissions' as blameable. There is also the fact that rôle-omissions, as they were earlier called, are very unlikely to be unintentional and are pretty well always blameable. As we are conceiving omissions, and as they will be defined in due course, it is possible that they be unintentional. Nothing much hangs on this decision, however.

This three-part division of intentions certainly does not apply to the acts which we compare with omissions. This is a considerable difference between act and omission. This may also come as a surprise, and indeed the surprise derives from a truth. If one takes any of the acts in our examples, say removing library books from poor schools, it is possible at least to imagine a related partly intentional action, and a related unintentional action. That is one fact. Another, however, is that our comparisons of act and omission invariably involve only fully intentional acts. That is our practice, how we go on. One difference between acts and omissions as we have them, then, is that the conceivable acts are fully intentional ones, and the omissions *may* be fully intentional, partly intentional or unintentional.

I trust there will be no suspicion that this distinction between acts and omissions is somehow arbitrary, or that it will have the effect of begging some question. It *is* a distinction between acts and omissions as we have them, between the actions which we relate as act and omission. In fact, as will become apparent, my conclusions do not depend greatly on the fact that all acts, unlike most of their related omissions, are fully intentional. More precisely, it is not greatly important to my conclusions that there are possible actions which in fact we do not consider but which stand to acts as partly intentional and unintentional omissions stand to fully intentional omissions.

(v) There is a related way in which some acts and omissions differ, having to do with the natures of their intentions. The intentions that would issue in the conceivable acts in the six examples are horrific or insane, inhuman, vicious, grasping, uncaring in the extreme. Let us give a moment or two to details of this intentionality. The agent, in the case of any of the conceivable acts, would be *aware* that there were victims of his act, persons at least badly affected by it. He would be aware that victims existed. In the case of some of the conceivable acts, the agent's awareness would derive from the fact that he would have to bring himself into the neighbourhood of the person or persons affected by his act. In the case of other acts the agent would necessarily have a lively awareness of the existence of victims without actually coming into their neighbourhood. This is true of the sending of the food parcel and, in different ways, of voting for the appalling party, evicting people for greater profits and contributing funds to a dictatorship.

It is worth noticing separately that in the conceivable acts the victims would be *individuated* by the agent. One way in which a victim is individuated, we can say, is by the agent knowing such individual features of the victim that the victim, for the agent, *is a person*. We might spend time making this notion more precise but it is not necessary. We can also allow another way of individuation, whereby groups of victims are known to the agent by shared features, perhaps connected with membership of a social class, which again makes them *persons* for the agent. As will be plain enough, individuation is something over and above just the awareness that victims do exist. There would be individuation in the case of all our six conceivable acts.

Let us compare this with the natures of the intentions in the case of the omissions or, more precisely, in the three cases of omissions. We must obviously distinguish between unintentional, partly intentional and fully intentional omissions.

Unintentional omissions, as we know, are actions such that neither the agent's immediate nor his earlier intentions involved the character or effect of his action taken as an omission. His intentions, then, are in no way suggested by this action taken as an omission. His immediate intention will have to do with his action taken as something other than the omission, perhaps buying a car or putting his money into a building society. It may be an intention of an ordinary or of course a good kind. In unintentional omission, there is no awareness of the existence of victims, no individuation of them.

To pass on to the nature of *fully intentional* omissions, there is unlikely to be an instance of any of the omissions in our six examples being performed in a fully intentional way. This is so, at least, if we take certain more precise versions of the examples. It is unlikely to happen that because of some extraordinary situation, a man fully believes that his omitting to contribute a certain sum to Oxfam on a particular day will result in the deaths of several people known to him, and he does do something or other rather than contribute, *and* he does this in the desire that the people die. That is, he has the intention of their deaths in the way that the related intention is had by the conceivable man who does the act of sending a poisoned food parcel. The omitter may not have it in mind to support his family or to do any such thing by his action. Such an omission would in fact derive from an intention about as horrific as the intention in the case of the related act. There would also be a similarity of intention in our other five examples. That is, the intention in the omission if it were fully intentional would be bad, and about as bad as the intention in the conceivable act.

There is a traditional problem about the nature of the intentions in partly intentional omissions, and the goodness or badness or whatever of the agents. What has been said here so far, not very usefully, is that the omissions derive in part from earlier intentions, which intentions have in them something of the character or effect of the omissions, in our examples a black character and effect.

We rightly feel that there is more, perhaps a good deal more, to be said against the man whose failure to contribute to Oxfam is partly intentional, as against the man whose failure is unintentional. There is, it seems, a very great deal less to be said against the man whose failure is partly intentional, as against the man whose failure is fully intentional. Still, how exactly are we to judge partly intentional omission? Reflection on the question leads in several directions. It does seem settled that there is a great difference between the earlier intentions and activity in the case of partly intentional omission and the intentions in either the related fully intentional omissions or of course the related acts. There is nothing less than a gap between not reading a newspaper account of a famine, albeit out of a certain selfish impulse to avoid the matter, and sending a poisoned food parcel or performing a certain conceivable omission with full intention. One can say that almost all partly intentional omissions reflect better or less badly on the agents than the related fully intentional omissions or the acts. This is partly a matter of the degree of awareness in the earlier intention of the existence of victims of the possible future omission. There is also a point to be made about individuation.

We shall later spend some more time on the subject of partly intentional omissions. For now, we have the comparison that in many cases of act and omission, the conceivable act would derive from an appalling or at least bad intention, while the omission if it is partly intentional derives from intentions which do not throw so bad a light on the agent. The comparisons with the fully intentional and the unintentional omissions are of less interest.

It is to be remembered, by the way, that not *all* cases of act and omission are like the six with which we began, where the intention in the act is as *bad* as in fully intentional omission, *worse* than in partly intentional and unintentional omission. Consider the three possible versions of an omission of a kind mentioned above, a doctor's not giving penicillin to an old, dying, suffering and incurable person. It may be that neither the omission if fully intentional, nor the related act of killing, comes from anything like a bad intention. Partly intentional omission would here be worse and indeed unthinkable, and unintentional omission worse and no doubt culpable. There are also other conceivable cases of act and omission which are different from our six.[3]

(vi) Let us turn from intentions and agents to customary morality, to ordinary judgements about the rightness or wrongness of actions. In the case not of all but of many acts, including all those in our six examples, there is a general acceptance that the act would be wrong, or worse than just wrong. There would also be a general acceptance that the related *fully intentional* omissions would be wrong. The same thing, whatever we are to make of the fact, is not true of the related partly intentional omissions.

The acts and the fully intentional omissions would be taken to offend against one or more rules, principles or laws. The act of contributing to a dictatorship would offend against fairly ordinary sorts of political principles, and no doubt against international declarations of human rights. So with the related fully intentional omission. The same and more is to be said of the conceivable act of voting for the appalling political party with the intention of keeping the lives of some people shorter. So with the related fully intentional omission. Removing library books from poor schools, and evicting families for private profit, and the related omissions, would offend at least against standards of ordinary decency or humanity. Infecting people would go against both ordinary morality and law, as with the related omission. The act of sending poisoned food parcels would outrage anything recognizable as a morality, and also be against ordinary law. So with the related fully intentional omission.

Whatever view we ourselves in this inquiry come to have of the rightness or wrongness of the related partly intentional omissions, then, they are not now accepted as wrong. It is not as if they go against ordinary political principles, or standards of ordinary decency, or ordinary morality, or ordinary law. What I have in mind is a matter of the non-existence of certain conceivable attitudes, practices and institutions, just as it is a matter of fact that the related actions and fully intentional omissions are accepted as somehow prohibited. Far from being prohibited, many of the omissions may well be accepted as required or obligatory. If I were to increase my contribution to Oxfam to the point where my children lived poorly, in comparison with certain other children in my society, I would run afoul of an established outlook. That outlook requires that I fulfil certain ordinary obligations, that I have and act on certain loyalties, and, in order to do such things, that I omit various other things.

There remain the unintentional versions of our six omissions. Ordinary morality obviously does not take them to be wrong. They are hardly distinguished from the partly intentional omissions.

3. Different comparisons

The following comparisons between act and omission, as we shall see, have another importance.

(vii) Acts and omissions give rise to what we have so far called results or effects, and might more precisely call main effects. These are usually the events or states mentioned or implied in the description of the action. In the six examples, they are the deaths of some people, shorter average lifetimes of some people, the states of health of certain people, poor education of certain children, homelessness of some families, and political oppression.

In general the main effects in question with acts and omissions are harms and benefits. Harms so-called are to be taken as including awfulnesses and catastrophes. The problem we are considering arises mainly from the fact that some harms arise from omissions, and so raise a question about whether the omissions are as wrong as certain terrible acts which would have similar or identical, similar or connected effects. There is also the problem, not illustrated by our six examples, that some benefits are as much the issue of terrible acts as they are of omissions, and so raise the question of whether the acts are right. The cases of killing or letting-die are central here.

Not much needs to be said of the nature of harms and benefits. It can be assumed that there is some fairly wide agreement about what states of affairs are to be avoided or prevented, if we can, and what states of affairs are to be secured, if we can. Such an agreement was assumed, of course, in my listing a moment ago of the harms involved in the six examples. There is a considerable problem, certainly, of what general and systematic summary can be given of such events or states. The answer which I favour is that benefits are states or events for which there is something to be said if one is committed to the well-being of everyone without exception, and to something of a related kind for other sentient things. Harms are characterized in terms of conflict with the same ideal. We can agree for the most part on what things are harms and what things are benefits without agreeing on the general systematic summary.

The principal point to be made about main effects has already been in view. It is that the main effect of an act may or may not be the very same as the main effect of the related omission. A comparison as to effects may produce a sameness or a difference between an act and the related omission. It is more likely that there will be a difference. This remains so even when the effect of the act can be described in the same words as the effect of the omission. Generally, of course, there is some *similarity* between the two main effects, which similarity leads to the two actions being brought together as act and omission. Occasionally, there is *connection* in main effect, not identity or similarity, as in a situation where a man's act will be the killing of one man and his omission will for some reason result in someone else's killing of twenty.[3]

Main effects, to repeat, are states or events mentioned or implied in the descriptions of actions. They are not to be taken as including effects on agents themselves unless this is specified. Nor do main effects include what may be called side-effects. We shall notice both these things separately.

(viii) Some acts make it more or less certain that main effects, whether harms or benefits, will occur. So with some omissions. For the most part, however, there is less than certainty. There is only probability, something in between zero and one. The principal fact to be noted, however, is that it may or may not be true that the probability of a main effect, given an act, is the same as the probability of a main effect, given the related omission. Usually the probability of the two possible effects is not the same. If the probability of an effect given an action is sometimes close enough to be indistinguishable from the probability of a similar or identical effect given the omission, the ordinary case is otherwise. A moment's attention to the examples indicates this. Again, it is a simple but important fact.

(ix) Connected with things already noticed, but distinct from them, are what we can call experiential effects on the agent. An act or an omission is within the experience of the agent, and hence has effects on him at the time and thereafter. These are likely to be different as between act and omission. The different emotional concomitants of killing as against letting-die may come to mind. One relevant fact in connection with the difference in experiential effects has to do with responses already mentioned having to do with attack and the like. However rational it may be, we have a *livelier* experience of attacking than of not-saving. A larger relevant fact is that our customary moralities, as we know, include prohibitions of many acts, and so give rise to accusation and self-accusation. What we feel when we remember our partly intentional omissions is different from what we would feel if we were to remember that we had performed the related acts. The difference in experiential effects, of course, will be different in the case of fully intentional as against partly intentional omissions, and so on.

(x) In addition to main effects, and experiential effects on agents, there are side-effects. These may be effects on victims, other than main effects, or they may be effects on third parties. Any of our examples can be used to illustrate the fact that the side-effects of an omission are likely to be different from the side-effects of a possible act. There are, for example, the side-effects on others in my life if I increase very greatly my contribution to Oxfam. These would be different, certainly, from side-effects of the conceivable act. In the second example there would be the side-effects on the economically worst-off tenths of there being a political party with the aim of keeping their average lifetimes shorter. There are possible economic side-effects to be taken into account with respect to our ordinary activities in omitting to work for a change in average lifetimes. So with our omissions and conceivable acts in connection with health, education, homelessness and political oppression.

The side-effects of a possible act, then, may be roughly the same as, but are likely to be different from, the side-effects of the omission. It is to be added, as in the case of main effects and experiential effects, that we are likely to have a situation of probabilities and of course different probabilities.

(xi) An agent who did act, rather than omit partly intentionally or unintentionally, would almost certainly put himself in a position different from the positions of others, partly in terms of experiential effects, partly in other ways. The others in question may be members of large classes, such as the class of adult and responsible members of a society, or smaller and better-defined classes, such as that of doctors. Omission of the unintentional and partly intentional kinds is the normal thing. The agent who acts thereby makes himself different, in particular insofar as experiential effects are concerned. He may, for example, take upon himself an unequal amount of guilt, however rational or irrational, if guilt is ever rational. The situation is quite different, incidentally, with rôle-omissions. There, not-acting is abnormal and unexpected, rather than acting, and it is omitters rather than doers who stand out.

Our eleventh comparison, then, comes to this: those who act, as against those who omit, almost certainly make themselves different or unequal in some class or classes of persons. The examples illustrate this.

Summary of Comparisons

(i) Act and omission are both actions
(ii) Omission likely to be described negatively, act affirmatively

(iii) Omission as causally efficacious as act, although other persons likely to contribute to main effect of omission
(iv) Act fully intentional, omission any of fully intentional, partly intentional or unintentional
(v) Intentions in many acts appalling; intentions in related partly intentional omissions tolerable
(vi) Most acts and fully intentional omissions customarily accepted as somehow wrong; not so the related partly intentional and unintentional omissions

---

(vii) Main effects of act and omission likely different
(viii) Probabilities of main effects likely different
(ix) Experiential effects likely different, and of different probabilities
(x) Side-effects likely different, and of different probabilities
(xi) Agent's situation likely unequal to that of others after act as against omission

4. What makes for rightness

We can now characterize an act and an omission of the kind with which we are concerned as (a) a pair of possible actions (b) taken as identical or similar in main effect, or at any rate connected, and such that (c) the act is fully intentional while the omission can be fully intentional, partly intentional or unintentional, and (d) the intentions in the two actions may be greatly different in nature. We might add something (e) which has been assumed and which will be of a bit of importance later, that the omission (which we are taking to be the omitting action, or what *was* done) must not involve less expenditure of energy or whatever than the omitted action, what was not done, would have. The omitting action of reading the newspaper at breakfast cannot count as the writing of a whole book.

Our first issue is whether *every* act and omission are factually different in a single way which makes for rightness. It seems that we can now settle that issue fairly quickly. Our inquiry, a pretty exhaustive one, has turned up *no* single difference of fact which holds between every act and omission without exception. The truth seems to be that when people consider two actions with related main effects, and distinguish them as act and omission, they sometimes do so on the basis of some criteria and sometimes on the basis of other criteria. There is no single general criterion. This is not all that unusual in conceptual and indeed practical life. We might describe the situation differently and with the appearance of greater neatness, of course. That is, we might choose to specify several different senses or sorts of act-and-omission, each tied to certain criteria only. There is not much to be gained by doing so.

Our inquiry has of course produced important differences holding between some or many acts and their related omissions, but, before proceeding to them, can we conclude more generally that there is no general difference of fact which gives rise to a general difference in rightness? Can we conclude that we have not missed anything?

The first of three things to be said about this is that no supporter of the idea that there is some general factual difference, one of moral relevance, has ever made clear what that difference is. This is telling. We are not examining a matter which is essentially obscure. What we are examining, once we have got rid of such light ideas as that we are dealing with an act on the one hand and a puzzling nothing on the other, or anyway an act and something greatly more indeterminate – what we are examining is two plainish things: two actions or action-sequences. Certainly they may raise great problems having to do with their main effects, experiential effects, side-effects and equality-effects, and they may be baffling or mysterious in these respects. Still, we know what sort of thing is in question in these respects. If there is *another sort of thing* on hand, why is it not produced? As David Hume may have remarked of philosophical circumstances like this one, a challenge unmet may come close enough to a proof.

A second consideration is one which should not escape the attention of anyone who thinks of a decently wide range of examples of act and omission. We are looking for a general difference between acts and omissions which supports a difference in rightness. One can look for such a thing with more hope if one supposes, very forgetfully, that there is at least *moral uniformity*, as we can call it, about acts and omissions: for example, at least a presumption of some kind that all omissions are better, somehow, than their acts. This is a non-starter. It sometimes seems to be half-forgotten that there are more cases of act and omission than problematic ones. The fact of the matter is that some conceivable *acts* are unquestionably better than some *omissions*. Whatever one's reluctance it is unquestionably better to act, where the act is the killing of one man oneself, if it really is true that the only alternative, one's not shooting, will have the certain effect that someone else will shoot twenty men. It follows that while we are looking for a general difference between acts and omissions, it is not one that is always morally *conclusive*, in the way of making omissions better. We are looking for a general difference which is of an *uncertain* moral effect. Such a thing is conceivable, but not much more.

There is one final consideration which I shall postpone for a bit, until after we have considered the non-general differences between acts and omissions. With the aid of that final consideration we shall conclude that there is in fact no entirely general difference between acts and omissions which gives rise to a difference in rightness.

Let us now consider the limited factual differences between acts and omissions which we came upon in our inquiry. Some of these give rise to differences in rightness, but which are they?

The first limited difference (ii) was that there is a tendency for omissions to be described negatively and acts to be described affirmatively. It is unthinkable that this linguistic difference in itself is such as to make an action right or wrong, or more right or more wrong. The presence of a 'not' or something like it in a description cannot itself be of moral relevance. One may feel that the linguistic fact is somehow relevant to the matter in hand. This comes about, presumably, not only because of its connection with rôle-omissions, but because it is connected with non-linguistic facts, to which we shall come, which are of relevance to rightness.

The next limited difference we came upon (iii) was basically that while each of an omission and an act is a necessary condition of its respective effect, it is usually the case that the omissions of other people are also necessary conditions of the omission's effect. Not only I but also others must fail to contribute to Oxfam in order for some persons to die. It cannot be, however, that my action can be made right, let us say, by the existence of others like it. There might be excuse for *me* in the fact of numbers, but it can hardly be that *what I do*, my action, is made right or better by it. By way of analogy, torturing would not be better if there were more torturers. Nor, by the way, does there seem any force in another mentioned aspect of connections between the actions and their results. If an action of mine could have prevented great distress, and did not, it cannot be that its status is improved by the fact that the distress would have occurred had I not existed.

What of (iv) the fact that the acts would be fully intentional and the omissions may be fully intentional or partly intentional or unintentional? Let us have in mind the particular comparison between acts and partly intentional omissions. These omissions are plainly of most relevance to us.

There are those who think, confusedly to my mind, that an act's being fully intentional and an omission's being partly intentional is of importance to the rightness or wrongness of the act and the omission. The kind or degree of intentionality makes the omission not wrong, or less wrong. There is a long tradition of commitment to such views and related ones, its greatest figure being Immanuel Kant. No doubt the tradition has things of value in it, but its central ideas are certainly not ours. That much can be shown, I think, simply by making some distinctions.

Our concern in all of this inquiry, as I remarked at the start, is the rightness and wrongness of actions. Our concern, at any rate fundamentally, is with kinds of conduct, not kinds of people. What is it for an action to be right? It is for it to be the action, of those which are possible, which can rationally be expected to give rise to the best state of affairs. Again, it is the action which would be selected by a knowing judge as likely to give rise to the best state of affairs. More might be said of such a man, but there is no possibility of giving a determinate account of his state of knowledge or his capability of judgement. The idea, roughly, is that his knowledge is as great as is humanly available at the time, and his judgement is the best available. In certain cases little knowledge will be available and the best judgement must be tentative or even hazardous.

As for the matter of good states of affairs, they can be as well or better described as states of experience, states involving amounts and distributions of experience. They do not have to do with any 'values' which are not such facts of experience, the experience of the agent and also others affected at the time and thereafter by his action. It may be wondered what 'values' are left out. If there is a fact about an action which in itself is not a fact of distress or frustration or enjoyment or enrichment, or any other kind of quality of experience, such a fact is not in itself of relevance to the rightness of actions. The bare facts, *taken as without effects in experience*, that an action is according to a rule, or that it is thought of in a certain way by the agent, are not of relevance.

What we have, to return to the main point, is that an action's rightness or wrongness is independent of the kind or degree of intentionality from which it issued. That an action was partly intentional, or fully intentional, or indeed unintentional, does not matter. It makes no difference to its rightness or wrongness. It is not that an omission as compared with an act is right or less wrong because the omission is partly intentional while the act would be fully intentional. There is a bit more to be said, however, and it will be best to proceed by considering at the same time our next limited difference (v). It was that the intentions in many conceivable acts would be appalling, while those in the related partly intentional omissions are something like tolerable. The intentions in the case of the conceivable acts in our examples would be horrific, inhuman, vicious, grasping or something of the sort. The intentions in the case of the related partly intentional omissions are not of these kinds. On the contrary, the *immediate* intentions may be good ones, such as the intention to safeguard the future of one's own children. The *earlier* intentions, whatever else is to be said of them, are greatly different in nature from the intentions in the case of the conceivable acts. They involve a lesser grasp of the effects of the relevant omissions.

None of this matters either to the question of rightness. As remarked at the start, an action can be right, one action which ought to have been done, although it was done from the wrong motive, and an action can be wrong, something that ought not to have been done, although it was done out of a good intention. Consider a member of the House of Commons who voted for the establishment of the National Health Service. We suppose that he did the right thing, that his action was right, even if he was in fact opposed to the idea on principle and voted for the Health Service only out of a completely self-serving intention to gain re-election. Or rather, as needs to be allowed, there are two propositions that can be expressed by saying that he did the right thing. The main one amounts to the proposition that his action was right, understood on the lines already suggested. It is true. The other is to the effect that *he* was true to his principles, and so on. It is false. If we are in fact concerned with his action's being right, however we may express this, his self-serving intention and his going against his principles is irrelevant.

It would be mistaken, of course, to suggest that the subject of agents and intentions is unimportant. On the contrary, if it is of secondary importance, it is nonetheless of great importance. It is of great importance to us since we want to have such people as will do the right thing. We are with every reason interested in the goodness or badness of people, as indicated by kind and nature of intentionality, since we are concerned with their future actions. The goodness or humanity or whatever of a person is our best guide to his future conduct. This, however, should not be confused with the idea that what makes an action right is even partly its actual intentionality, the kind and nature of intentionality actually involved. The fact that we have a great concern with how intentional a man's action was and what his intention was, because of our concern about future actions, should not be confused with the mistake that what makes an action right is the intentionality behind it. That question, the rightness of the action, is not touched by the agent's intentions having been what they were, although the action will no doubt indicate at least something about his intentions, and his intentions will tell us something about his likely future behaviour. It is irrelevant to the question of the rightness of the M.P.'s action in voting for the National Health Service that his action, taken with a knowledge of his principles, tells us something of his actual intentions and that those tell us something of his likely future activity.

It may be wondered for a moment if I am really describing *the action that turned out best*, and misappropriating the term 'right action' for it, while the right action is in fact the action done from a good intention and so on. Some will say that the correct description of the situation is that the M.P. did the wrong thing, or acted wrongly, and, as it happened, this turned out well. There is nothing unusual in that, they will say.

I am not in fact confusing the right action with what turned out best. The right action, to repeat, is the one which at the time would rationally have been judged as the one giving rise to the best state of affairs. It is obvious, then, that the right action is not necessarily the action that turns out best in fact, even in the short run. Nor is there any reason to think that our common notion of the right action can somehow be reduced to that. Even knowledgeable judges make mistakes.

What has been said in definition of right actions does bring into view another indubitable connection between the conception of a right action and that of intention. It too needs to be seen clearly for what it is and for what it is not. Given what has been said, the very definition of a right action brings in a notion of intention. That is, to re-write a bit, the right action is the one which would be favoured by a knowing judge *with a certain intention*: the intention to secure the best state of affairs. There is no doubt about that. There remains the different and essential point that it does not follow that a man's act is right, or wrong, if *he* acted out of this or that intention. The M.P.'s act was right in that it would have been favoured by a knowing judge with a certain intention. It does not follow, as we know, that it was wrong because the M. P. did not have an identical intention. If, on the contrary, the M. P. had had an identical intention, and acted as he did, that fact of *his* intention would not have made his act right either, as in fact it was.

One final remark. It may be allowed that a clear enough conception has been suggested, and that we can indeed consider the question of whether actions are right or wrong in the given way. But it may be wondered if this question is the fundamental question in morality, or indeed in life. The reply must be that there is no forcing anyone to be most concerned with what is right, with what ought to happen. Most of us *are* primarily so concerned, rather than with the question of an agent's actual intention taken by itself, or his moral standing taken by itself, or any other moral question. That is as much as can be said, and of course it is enough.

We were considering two questions. One was the question of whether our actual partly intentional omissions can be regarded as better than certain conceivable wrong acts because those acts would be fully intentional. The answer is no. The kind of degree of intentionality of an action makes no difference to its rightness or wrongness. Nor, to turn to the second question, does the nature of intentions matter. Whatever is to be said of the agent, an act is not made right by a good intention or wrong by a bad one. If it appears that these conclusions can be overturned, this will be no more than appearance, since it will be owed to giving a different definition or sense to 'the right action', 'what ought to be done' and so on. This is possible, certainly, but the resulting subject-matter is not ours, and not the fundamental subject-matter in moral and political reflection, whether carried on in books or in the rest of life.

The next difference between some acts and omissions (vi) has to do with accepted or ordinary morality. There, there is a distinction between the conceivable acts and fully intentional omissions on the one hand, and, on the other hand, the partly intentional and the unintentional omissions. The former are wrong, the latter not so. In particular, our ordinary failure to contribute to famine relief, or to political movements against dictatorships, is not wrong, but our related conceivable acts would be wrong. One point here is that it would just beg the question with which we are concerned if ordinary morality were taken without reflection to be correct. Certainly we are in no way forced to follow ordinary morality. It in no way follows from something's being generally accepted at a time that it is right. It does not follow from there being an accepted prohibition of the acts but not of the omissions that the omissions are better than the acts. What one needs to do, if one is doubtful about this proposition, is to think of the history of morality. It is a history of what we cannot take to be other than mistakes, a history of beliefs that were both mistaken and generally accepted.

We can allow, perhaps, that something or other is to be said for a generally accepted view, but it is certainly obscure what it is. It is certain that we shall not come to have a very important consideration. The obscure recommendation of ordinary morality is not enough to put into question our conclusion that ordinary morality is mistaken in the matter of the connection between intentionality and the worth of omissions and acts. We can also allow a second thing. It is that if people do have certain moral attitudes, however right or wrong those attitudes are, denials of them may result in hurts and distresses. If I believe that you ought to do something for me, the fact that I am mistaken does not stop my being hurt or distressed by your not doing the thing. This sort of thing is sometimes of some importance. It is not of much importance here.

Things are different with all the remaining comparisons on our list, all of them involving limited differences between acts and omissions. All of these comparisons are of clear importance to the rightness or wrongness of actions.

It is inescapable (vii) that the harms and benefits that may result from acts and omissions are of importance to the moral assessment of those actions. This follows directly from what has been said about rightness. If considerations of death, distress and inequality do not enter into the judgement of the rightness or wrongness of acts and omissions, then nothing does. Some have tried to avoid the conclusion which follows, that *differences* in harms and benefits must therefore give rise to differences in rightness and wrongness between acts and omissions. They have tried to avoid the conclusion that it is more wrong to have two people suffering to a given extent, or indeed a thousand, than one person suffering to just that extent. Obviously there is no avoiding it. Great tragedies are more terrible than small, and still more to be avoided. We can say, in connection with this seventh comparison, that when other things are equal we are justified in omission rather than act if the omission involves the lesser harm or the greater benefit, and vice versa.

The eighth comparison is a relevant one. An act carrying a high probability of harm, other things being equal, is worse than an omission carrying a lower probability of an identical harm, and vice versa. There are a number of related propositions about probability. An omission carrying a certain low probability of a certain greater harm may be worse than an act carrying a certain high probability of a certain lesser harm, and so on.

The ninth fact of acts and omissions, their experiential effects, is also morally relevant. In certain instances these effects may be of decisive moral importance. In other instances, perhaps more, they are less important than other things. Side-effects, the subject of our tenth comparison, are also morally relevant, and perhaps likely to be more important than experiential effects. Finally, it is clear enough that the eleventh comparison, having to do with the position of the agent in some class of comparison, is of relevance. There are some actions which a man might contemplate, and which it would be wrong for him to do because of the extent to which he would be made unequal as a result.

5. Our six omissions

We now have a grasp of the comparisons between acts and omissions. Let us turn back to the particular omissions and conceivable acts with which we began. Would the acts be worse than the omissions are? Would they be no worse? We should now be able to decide. If they would be no worse, the violent have truth on their side in the claim that our ordinary law-abiding conduct is wrong. Their *tu quoque*, whatever is to be said of the relevance of such retorts, is not to be put aside as a falsehood or a mistake. Let us get the answer to our question.

We have spoken of 'the omission of not sending what money we could to Oxfam' and the conceivable act of 'sending poisoned food parcels to India'. There was also the omission in which we 'fail to contribute funds to political movements against dictatorships', and the conceivable act in which we 'contribute funds to a dictatorship'. These easy phrasings may lead one to overlook what has not been overlooked in our survey, that omissions and acts can differ in main effects. They can differ, as already remarked, even when two different main effects fall under the same piece of language, the same description. Certainly that is clear enough when one stops to think. On the other hand it is possible that omissions and acts be identical in main effects. There is precisely the same situation with the other important comparisons (viii to xi) between acts and omissions. There can be difference or sameness with respect to probability of main effect, and with respect to experiential effects, side-effects, equality-effects and the probabilities of each of these.

There is another fact, a connected one, which is fundamental. *We can choose what conceivable actions to compare with our actual omissions.* Given an actual omission, the related conceivable act is not thereby determined. There is not *one* conceivable action which is the act for that omission. In fact there is no fixed answer, or rather, there is *no answer*, to this question: what is *the* conceivable act which stands to a particular omission? Habit, customary examples, and simple situations may lead us to suppose that there is an answer, but they mislead us. We choose which possible act goes with an omission, what to compare with what. We can vary examples in order to find things out. We have a freedom of inquiry.

Perhaps the tendency of my argument will now be anticipated. *We tend to think that conceivable acts would be worse than our omissions because we have in mind certain of those conceivable acts rather than others. If we think of others, there is the plain conclusion that our omissions are as wrong as those acts. Those acts would be terribly wrong.*

Consider once again the first of the six examples as it was given. In thinking of it, we are very likely indeed to have in mind several ideas. One is that sending poisoned food would not merely probably but almost certainly have a terrible main effect, deaths that otherwise would not happen, while not contributing to Oxfam would probably have *some* terrible main effect, some number of deaths that otherwise would not happen, not necessarily the same number of like deaths. Here there is a difference in main effects, and also in their probabilities. As for the remaining three comparisons, we are likely to think of worse experiential effects for the agent in the case of the conceivable act, worse side-effects, and a worse equality-situation. There can then be no surprise in the fact that we have a strong inclination to think of the conceivable act as worse than our actual omission.

There is another comparison. Let us fix in our minds a conservative estimate of the whole upshot of an actual omission and then conceive of an act of the same upshot. How much could I contribute to Oxfam next year? Let us say £4,000. Suppose I do not give the money. It is a secure judgement, surely, that my not doing so will have at least two deaths as its very probable main effect. Let us say, for purposes of argument, that the probability is 75 per cent. The *experiential effects* on me of not doing so will be, very probably, small. My own *equality-situation*, vis-à-vis those of people like me in my society, will be pretty well unaffected by my omission. The *side-effects* of my omission will be considerable: they will include the effects of what I do instead with the £4,000, and also the effects of the two deaths. Suppose, for purposes of argument, that the money will be spent on improving the life of myself and my family. These improvements, by way of certain comparisons between societies, will provide what indubitably must count as indulgences and luxuries for myself and my family. The effects on people related to the two who die will be very different of course.

It is conceivable that I arrange to perform a certain act, perhaps a poisoning, carrying a 75 per cent probability of the deaths of two persons. If I were to do so freely, the experiential effects on me might very probably be small, not different from those of my actual omission. Let us have precisely this possibility as to experiential effects in mind. I would not then be the person I now am, of course, subject to certain feelings of guilt and so on. Let us suppose also that the side-effects by way of the two deaths would be the same as before. That is, we suppose it is by my act that I and my family have £4,000 worth of indulgences, and that there are the same side-effects as before by way of the deaths of the victims. Let us suppose, finally, for reasons which we can conceive, that my own equality-situation in my life would be the same as in the case of my actual omission. Certainly we have now conceived of an entirely extraordinary situation, one that is certain never to obtain. That does not matter at all for the argument. What matters is the likeness of this merely conceivable act to my actual omission, and what we say about the conceivable act.

What we must say, of course, is that my conceivable act would be wrong, and thus we come to the conclusion that my omission next year will be precisely as wrong. We come to the general conclusion that our ordinary lives consist in omissions as wrong as certain conceivable terrible acts. Only quite different conduct, of a kind sometimes mistakenly put aside as something for saints, would be right.[4] It is to be allowed, of course, that my spending the £4,000 on myself and my family will only be as wrong as the one conceivable act. It is not that it will be as wrong as some multitude of conceivable acts each similar in upshot to one of the multitude of omissions I will perform in spending the £4,000 as I shall. It does not follow from the fact that my doing *A* was also not doing a thousand other things, that I could have done the thousand things. That does not much reduce the gravity of our general conclusion.

Is it reduced, incidentally, by the objection that my omission will be only about half as wrong as the conceivable act, since the conceivable act would also be something else: an omission to contribute?[5] My spending £4,000 on myself and my family, it may be objected, is only harmful as an omission, but the act of poisoning would be harmful both as that act and also as an omission, the omission of not contributing money to Oxfam. The act of poisoning would be about twice as wrong.

There are possible situations in which an objection of this kind is in place, not that its conclusion is greatly reassuring. (The omission in those situations, it might be replied to the objector, is *fully half as wrong* as some terrible act.) The objection is in fact not relevant to our argument. This is so for the reason that the act of poisoning would not necessarily count as a relevant omission. It would not count, for example, as omitting to contribute £4,000 to Oxfam. This follows from our conception of acts and omissions. An action is a given omission only if what was not done could have been done with no greater expenditure of energy, resources or whatever than that expended in what was done. My reading a newspaper for a few moments cannot count as omitting to write a book. My conceivable act of poisoning, to return to that, would not necessarily be anything at all like omitting to contribute £4,000 to Oxfam.

6. Conclusion defended

The conclusion that our ordinary omissions are terribly wrong depends on there being no differences between acts and omissions other than those already listed. It depends on its being true, more particularly, that there is no general factual difference between acts and omissions. Two arguments were given against there being such a thing, and a third promised. It can now be provided.

If the factual difference exists, then even if it escapes our detection or description, we ought to be able to feel its moral effect. We ought to be aware of its effect in terms of the rightness or wrongness of actions. Such responses could not possibly be a matter of the special capabilities of only certain persons. Morality is not E. S. P. The difficulty, of course, is that we have to be sure, about any example, that we are not in fact responding to relevant differences of the kinds we now know, such as difference in probability of main effect.

We can devise certain examples, in areas less controversial than those we have been considering, and hence where we are less likely to go wrong, and with these examples it is impossible to have any feeling of difference in rightness between act and omission. The examples, of course, will be such that there is no difference of the kinds so far allowed to be relevant. We can proceed by way of a euthanasia example. There is the possible act, which might be a doctor's turning off a tap in a blood transfusion tube. The patient, who is incurable and in torment, dies. There is the possible omission, which might again be not providing penicillin for pneumonia. Again the patient would die. *If* we hold the act and omission identical in the relevant ways of which we know, it will surely be impossible to achieve any sense of difference in rightness between the two actions. Certainly it is not hard to drift into the feeling that there is more to be said for the omission. It seems invariably true that if this is done at all reflectively, it is done by changing the example: that is, by *not* holding the two actions identical in the five relevant ways of which we know. The temptation, if that is what it is, seems near to irresistible. In my view all recent philosophers who have tried to claim a special moral difference between acts and omissions have fallen prey to the temptation, or anyway not taken good care to have their examples satisfy the condition of having act and omission alike in the given ways. If the two actions are really held identical in the given ways, I propose, we cannot achieve any real sense of moral difference between them.

Some will suppose there is another way of resisting the general conclusion that in our ordinary omissions we do wrong to a terrible extent. They will suppose that the conclusion can be refuted or put into question by this argument: if the conclusion were true, we would be moral monsters; the wrongfulness of our actions would surely support this conclusion about ourselves; we are not moral monsters; indeed, it would not make sense to claim this of all of us; therefore the conclusion that we all do wrong to a terrible extent is mistaken or somehow in question.

The issues raised are large ones, and I shall do no more than quickly suggest reasons for thinking that the objection fails.

It has already been remarked that it does not follow directly from an action's being right that it preserves the agent's moral standing. Nor does it follow directly from an action's being wrong that it reduces or destroys the agent's moral standing. Still, from an act's being wrong together with certain other facts it does follow that the agent is open to question, or worse than that. What can be said in the case of our omissions?

It is to be kept in mind, first, that few if any of us omit to contribute to Oxfam in anything remotely like the fully intentional way. We do not *aim* at causing death. There are no *such* monsters. Secondly, are there only a few people, as may be thought, whose omissions are of the opposite kind, wholly unintentional? Are there only a few, that is, who have not earlier taken avoiding action? There are more of these innocents than might be supposed, at least if one gives a certain characterization of what is required for partly intentional omission.

It is reasonable to say that for something to count as an earlier intention-to-avoid, the person in question needs to have had more than fragmentary ideas in mind for a moment, more than a flicker of images. The person in question needs to have had a decent awareness of the relevant effects of the later omission. Also, he needs to have had a decent awareness of what he might do instead in the future. There are many people who have too small a conception of what might be called their world of possible effectiveness. They do not suppose, for example, that they can do anything to contribute to less inequality in average lifetimes. Nor can they be censured for their weak grasp of their possibilities of action. There are therefore more of the innocent, the unintentional, than might be supposed.

Consider now the moral standing of the partly intentional. Putting something out of mind in the required sense is likely to require self-deception. This cannot consist, as some philosophers seem to believe, in successfully lying to oneself, and therefore in believing both *p* and *not-p* together. Self-deception, at any rate when it is non-pathological, consists rather in an avoidance of evidence, or of pointers or clues, with the aim of *avoiding* belief. It consists in *persisting with a question*, which is better than getting a particular answer. Part of what enters into putting something out of mind, then, is the fact that we have kept a good distance from places of evidence, perhaps evidence about average lifetimes in developed societies, or the state of education in certain sorts of school. (I have not said enough, of course, to give the reality of all this. There are many ways and styles of avoiding evidence.) To come to the essential claim, there is some exculpation possible for typical self-deceivers. If I have the belief that a terrible state of affairs exists, about which I could do something, that is different from my in fact having a question about such a state of affairs.

There is something else to be said of partly intentional omission. Omitting to contribute to Oxfam, to the extent that one is in a state of belief, is likely to involve beliefs as to *distant* awfulness. It cannot be true that an act or omission is right or wrong because of its *spatial* relation to its result. It cannot be that our moral obligations are in any way a function, simply, of mileage. But the question of acts is not the question of agents, and the question of agents is not easy. What about the relevance of distance, in the ordinary sense and also others, to our standing as moral agents or as human? It seems to be true that those who drop bombs are less morally revolting, if those are the right words, than those who do the close work of hand-to-hand killing. Again, one would feel differently about a family, say, who let a man starve to death in their own flat, as against a family who failed to send food to a man known by them to be dying in another country. What I want to suggest, then, is that the fact that the victims of omissions are distant does have some exculpating effect with respect to agents.

Further and finally, with respect to partly intentional omission, it is safe to say that *in ordinary morality* it is as if there were some great difference of fact between acts and partly intentional omissions. This is a common belief or conviction. In ordinary morality, further, there is no awareness of the great wrongfulness of our ordinary omissions. These are both mistakes, I think, but they are not mistakes to which moral blame attaches. It is not a general requirement of being a good person, now, that one does not make these mistakes.

I take it that these various considerations go some considerable way towards *exculpating* many people. Or, to come to safer ground, and all the ground I need, it seems that the considerations do the lesser thing of *absolving most people from being moral monsters*. Whether exculpation, or the lesser absolving, it is partly something that is true at this time in human history. It is dependent on a certain general awareness at this time. It is not an exculpation or absolving that will persist, as it is, into the future. One may wonder, of course, whether it may apply *now* to oneself, but that is something else.

We were considering the argument that if we in our omissions do wrong to a terrible extent, we are moral monsters; and we are not such, and so it cannot be that we do wrong to a terrible extent. The reply has been that for various reasons a general and substantial proposition about overwhelming guilt on the part of many people does not follow from, and hence cannot endanger, the conclusion about the great wrongfulness of our omissions. It is not entirely clear that the conclusion would in fact *be* endangered if it did carry the given large consequence, but I leave the matter there.

7. Tu quoque

By our ordinary omissions we do as wrong as we might by certain awful acts. Some of us or indeed most of us will pay this conclusion no serious attention. Perhaps it is true that no one will take it so seriously as to act upon it. Such results are dispiriting only to those who are unaware of the history of political philosophy, of serious moral protest and of like things. Virtually every outlook or institution or practice which is now venerated did in fact begin life as a silly proposition upon which no one acted. It began life as such a proposition although in fact there was enough argument for it, and not enough against it.

What we must accept, to look back to the beginning of our inquiry, is that those who engage in violence of the Left have a truth on their side when they respond to the charge that *they* do wrong with the retort that *we* do wrong. What is to be said of this *tu quoque*? I supposed in the beginning that it cannot be put aside, and promised to return to the matter.

Overstatement is possible. Some of the violent will say that in fact they are not limited to the *tu quoque*, whatever it comes to. There is more. They will say that our ordinary contribution to the frightful circumstances of shorter lifetimes, miseries and the want of freedoms does not issue only in the judgement that we do wrong, and whatever follows from that, but also in the judgement that *our ordinary condemnation of violence is incoherent*. If this is not neatly expressed by those who defend their violence, that is in a way not unusual, and in a way not essential. It is not unusual for those who act in certain causes to be unable to do well in arguing for those causes; their being unable to do so is not essential to those causes being defensible ones. Policemen and soldiers should come to mind.

The claim by the violent that our condemnation of violence is incoherent proceeds as follows. We judge our kind of conduct to be right, and the conduct of the violent to be wrong, but the two kinds of conduct are alike in a certain fact, and this fact of likeness is all-important. Each kind of conduct consists in *the denial of human needs and indeed of life*. On the one hand these things are denied to the primary victims of acts of violence, and also in part to secondary victims, principally the families of primary victims. Whatever else is added, this much must be allowed. On the other hand, as has just been said, there are the innumerable victims of those of us who live ordinary law-abiding lives. They live less long, and badly, and without full freedom. On each hand, then, there is the denial of human needs and life. It is also true that while the two kinds of conduct are alike in the given fact, there is no relevant way in which our ordinary conduct is different from that of the violent, no difference which makes our conduct right and that of the violent wrong. We know there is no such difference in the fact that our ordinary conduct consists of omissions and the conduct of the violent consists of acts. *There is the result that our ordinary condemnation of violence is incoherent, that we fail to make what can count as judgements at all.* Our utterances are as insubstantial as those of a man who 'describes' an object in a certain way, perhaps as being of a certain colour, simply and solely because it has a quality to which he points, and then gives a contradictory description of another object with precisely the same quality. He has, in the most important sense of the words, said nothing at all.

The argument does not work, and in fact it overlooks plain things established in our reflections on acts and omissions. We have found that there are conceivable acts which are factually like our own omissions in all the relevant ways. Our omissions, therefore, are on a level of wrongness with these acts. None of that, however, goes any way towards establishing that our omissions are in the relevant ways like *the acts of the violent*. That is another matter. There is in fact no likelihood that our omissions can be shown to be like acts of the violent in main effect, or probability of it, or side-effects and their probability, and so on. The claim of incoherence can in fact be defeated by pointing out that it is just mistaken to say that our ordinary conduct is in no relevant ways different from that of the violent. It *is* different in ways in which omissions may differ from acts.

The violent, then, have only their *tu quoque*, and not the claim of incoherence. But is there something, perhaps much, to be said for the *tu quoque*?

The violent, when they are taxed with what will be called the irrelevance of their claim that our ordinary conduct is wrong, can maintain the strong truth that our two kinds of conduct are connected. It is not that the terrible circumstances of misery and injustice, against which violence is directed, come about by chance. They have not come about through historical passages in which we and our predecessors have played no particular part. The circumstances of misery and injustice, rather, are as good as our own work. We contribute to them essentially by our wrongful conduct. It is not that there is no connection between violence and our omissions, but rather that there is the connection that our omissions are essential contributions to the misery and injustice against which violence of the Left is directed.

More can be said along these lines, but all of it may get the reply that it is nothing to the point. Our ordinary omissions, it will be said, are not the subject-matter. The subject-matter is violence and what is to be said for and against it. It may be that there is the claimed connection between our omissions and the violence, and, for purposes of argument, it can be granted that our conduct is wrong. It is nonetheless true that the subject-matter is what it is, and that it is not our omissions.

There is only one proper judgement on this dispute. It is that there is no ordained subject-matter. There is *never* an ordained subject-matter. At bottom the criterion of relevance for any discussion is fixed by the demands of those who are taking part in it. If they cannot agree, they cannot discuss. No doubt anything which is one discussion remains within some wide boundary. No doubt it is true, too, that fact and logic impose requirements of appositeness on answers to particular questions, replies to particular claims. There is no fact of the world, however, and no consideration of logic, which stands in the way of the demand of the violent to bring our omissions into the discussion. It is not an absurd demand. What can stand in the way of it is only an opposed demand.

My own determination will by now be clear enough. It is that the discussion be the wider one. My first reason is that it seems possible that we proceed in too simple a way if we declare that the wrongfulness of violence is in no way diminished by the wrongfulness of our omissions. No doubt it is worth someone's while to say that two wrongs do not make a right. It may also be worth saying that there is reason to be sceptical, or perhaps it would be better to say that there is reason for some reserve, in a certain kind of situation. It is the kind of situation where we have one man's judgement on another's conduct, and the first man may be influenced by an unhappy perception of his own relation to the other's conduct. More particularly, we have some awareness that we make our necessary contributions to the circumstances which have led and continue to lead to violence. It seems to me a likelihood that this awareness affects our condemnations. Our condemnations, although condemnations still, are likely to be different if we are more aware of our own conduct and its wrongfulness.

There are two more reasons for the wider discussion. One is that it is in fact more important that *we* change our ways than it is that the violent change theirs. We do greatly more damage. Another lesser but good reason for the wider discussion is that it may do a little to diminish violence. The narrower discussion, rightly, has less chance.

3 ON TWO PIECES OF REASONING ABOUT OUR OBLIGATION TO OBEY THE LAW

All of us, save some true anarchists, have the conviction that the members of a society have some obligation to abide by the laws. At any rate, there is this obligation if the society is at all tolerable, which is to say that it has risen above barbarism, ancient or modern. Many things are not to be done, for a reason having to do with the fact that they are illegal, as distinct from other reasons which may also exist. It is thought by some that this obligation to keep to the laws is at its strongest with respect to the laws prohibiting violence. Still, it is quite unclear from what it is that the general obligation derives, and hence what weight it has. Almost all of us accept the existence of *political obligation*, as it happens to be called, partly because it may also be put as an obligation to the state or to government. Still, we are likely to grant that there are circumstances even in tolerable and better societies when the obligation is rightly overridden.

Of the long welter of doctrines whose aim has been to maximize or to minimize the fact of political obligation, I should like to consider two which are recent and, in the view of some, culminating. Both are developed reasonings of the kind mentioned in passing in the first essay of this book.[1] The first is partly to the effect that to accept political obligation, understood in a certain way, is in fact to be immoral. It is to go against a certain moral imperative. The second is partly to the effect that political obligation, differently understood, must be recognized as weighty. While one may in extraordinary circumstances be enabled to escape the obligation to the extent of engaging in the mildness of civil disobedience, or in what is called conscientious refusal, anything more is as good as unthinkable.

The first doctrine, owed to Robert Paul Wolff, comes of one of the traditions of thought and feeling which give first place to conscience and individual responsibility, and second place to political obligation and the like.[2] What is said about the immorality of political obligation is taken to have consequences for a particular idea of violence, one called the distinctive political concept of violence. We shall consider that matter, which is intimately related, as well.

The second doctrine, owed to John Rawls and much discussed by philosophers, derives from the tradition which has to do with suppositions about a social contract and about obligations which flow from it.[3] However, it is different from all or many of its predecessors. One large difference is that we are offered not only an argument about political obligation, and in particular our obligation not to use violence, but also an argument for two basic moral principles for the ordering of societies.

We shall not ignore the second argument since it is, in fact, of direct relevance to one of the fundamental difficulties encountered in reflection on political violence. This is the difficulty, of which something was said at the end of the first essay in this book, of settling on basic moral principles. We shall, then, consider not only certain specific contentions about a social contract and political obligation but also the argument for two basic moral principles, and the principles themselves.

Finally, by way of introduction to these two doctrines, it is to be said that they appear in one respect similar. They are complex, if in different ways. Their complexity, if I am right, is a false one. The fundamental argument, in each case, is relatively simple in kind, however compelling or uncompelling. An examination of the two doctrines, then, may serve to engender or strengthen a certain scepticism about what might be described as The Impressive in political argument. This scepticism, I am sure, in consideration of violence and other matters of seriousness, is an essential. Matters of seriousness call for a certain kind of plainness, and they generally have in them quite enough of true and unavoidable complexity. Certainly this is true of political violence.

My intentions in summary, then, are to consider a rejection of political obligation, to consider an acceptance of it and a related argument for two moral principles, and to raise a scepticism. The smallest intention is not the last one. To try to realize it, I shall linger a bit at points in the discussion rather than press on single-mindedly.

1. A right to obedience

Wolff's essay 'On Violence' has to do with the idea, as it may be expressed, and as he does express it, that some governments or states have *authority*. Some governments or states, to put the same thing differently, have a right to be obeyed by their subjects, the members of the relevant societies. This appears to be tantamount to the proposition which is our concern, that the subjects have an obligation to obey the law.

The obligation depends on the existence of law, as already remarked, and hence also on the existence of government and presumably society. The *reason* for the obligation has to do essentially with law, government and society. Political obligation, so-called mainly for this, is thus distinct from other obligations. If a man wounds another, in most circumstances, it will be at least possible that he has broken two obligations. One, we may say, is the simple obligation not to wound others. He would have this obligation even in a 'state of nature'. He would have it, that is, even if there were no law, in the ordinary sense, against his action. In addition to this, there is what is relevant to our present reflections, his obligation not to break the law against wounding others.

Political obligation is obviously a kind of moral obligation, although not the most familiar kind. The idea is that the subjects of governments, or some governments, are under some moral obligation to give up all courses of action which are made illegal. There is a moral restraint or prohibition on subjects with respect to these courses of action which are prohibited by the law of the state. Subjects are in some degree constrained to give up the behaviour in question, despite the fact that some of it may be morally desirable in their view.

The idea that subjects have an obligation, that governments have an authority, has been defended in different ways in the history of political thought. A conclusion about authority is accepted today by those of us who are committed, happily or unhappily and more or less completely, to a kind of government described by ourselves as democratic and by some others as bourgeois-democratic. It has been accepted by those who have made use of the notion of a social contract, as we know, by those who have believed in a monarch's divine right to rule, and by those who have found a superiority for a social or an economic class in the wisdom of the class or in what may be called its historical rôle or mission.

There is a good deal more to be said about the nature of political obligation, but let us now pass on to a second thing in 'On Violence'. The *distinctive political concept of violence*, like other concepts of violence, is said to be an idea of a use of force to effect decisions against the desires of others. That all concepts of violence have these features seems mistaken, but the matter is not important. The special feature of distinctively political violence is that it is a use of force either prohibited or not authorized (we are offered these two different possibilities) *by a state which has authority*. It is a use of force prohibited, to remain with that possibility, by a state whose subjects are under an obligation to obey its commands.

Let us look, thirdly, at a very different claim which enters into the argument. It is one to which Immanuel Kant gave some attention in his moral philosophy, and it is that a man is under an obligation not to act in a given way unless he himself sees good reason for so doing. The principal part of what is meant here is that a man is obliged not to act on the mere ground that someone has told him to do so. I do not have a reason for action in the bare fact that someone has told me to do whatever it is.

This seems a defensible claim, although it is inexplicit as it stands, and perhaps is in need of qualification. If we were to consider qualification, we should have to look into the possibility that unless we are all to become a good deal more reflective than we are, or more inactive, the range of acts for which good moral reason is needed must be limited. Humming a bit of a song while walking across a field with someone may not seem to be something that requires any reason. Certainly I am not prohibited from doing so by the fact that all I have in the forefront of my mind is that my companion has asked me to do the thing. Or, should we say that one's unconsidered recognition that certain behaviour is inconsequential *does* provide one with a good reason for the behaviour? In any case there is also consequential behaviour to consider. If I lack the slightest notion of what will avert some disaster, I am surely permitted to do what I am told by someone who has a gleam of hope in his eye. I am under no obligation not to act. Given these several reflections, it seems that a man can fulfil his obligation and still come pretty close to doing something simply because he has been told to do it. No doubt the ordinary case is different.

Let us now assemble our three pieces, unfinished as they are, and see how they work. There is an obligation just mentioned not to perform many actions, or many actions in certain settings, without what seems to be a good reason. This excludes doing many things simply because one has been told to do them. Well then, no state or government can have authority, the authority mentioned above. There is an obligation borne by every man which makes it impossible for any state to possess a certain right to a man's obedience. Or rather, to include a qualification to which we shall return, no state which is a practical possibility can ever have the right in question. It is allowed that it might be possessed by a certain ideal democratic state – ideal in that all its policies are considered and voted on by all its citizens and hence have their unanimous support. Such a state is allowed to be a fantasy.

If no state that is practically possible can have the given right to a man's obedience, there are consequences for the distinctive political concept of violence. If violence is taken to be a use of force prohibited by a state with the authority in question, then *there is no violence*, since there is no such state to prohibit anything. No use of force falls under the distinctive political concept of violence. The concept is empty. In order to get to a still further conclusion that is drawn, that talk of violence of this kind is *incoherent*, one notices the presupposition that the concept does distinguish between uses of force that are violent and uses of force that are not. This is a presupposition of an entirely general kind, present in the use of any concept. However, by the argument just given, the concept we are considering fails to do any such distinguishing. No use of force is

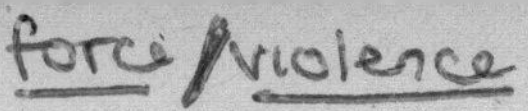

violent. Here we have incoherence, presumably related to inconsistency. Given the further argument that I intend, there will be no need for greater precision on this obscure point.

Incidentally, one can also attempt to establish the conclusion about incoherence from the other definition of violence. There, to recall, it is a use of force *not authorized*, as distinct from *prohibited*, by a state with the right kind of authority. In this case, since every use of force is *not authorized* by such a state, there being no such state, we may try to maintain that *every* use of force, however 'official', is an instance of violence, and also maintain the further conclusion about incoherence. Let us continue to have in mind the other form of the argument, proceeding from the definition of violence as a *prohibited* use of force.

2. Clarifications

What we now have is less than crystal clear. Still, it is clear enough that the argument so far does not have as its goal a merely conceptual point, a point about the emptiness or incoherence of a concept. To describe the argument this recherché way is entirely misleading. Its goal, rather, is a proposition of morality. The argument so far, at bottom, is something like this:

1. Each of us is obliged never to act, except perhaps in certain circumstances, on the mere ground that we have been told to do so.
2. Therefore, it is mistaken to think that any existing government could have a certain right to the obedience of its subjects.
3. One cannot claim, then, against those who do such things as set bombs, that they are violating a related obligation of obedience.

There is no reason to rewrite this latter conclusion in any less overt way. Consider an analogy. Suppose that one comes to believe, along with those impressed by the privacy of the soul, that it is impossible ever to assess a man's responsibility for an action. Whether he *really* had a choice must remain obscure. Suppose one believes, too, that it is necessary, if punishing a man is to be morally tolerable, that it be known that he was in fact responsible to some degree for an offence. There follows the conclusion that no one ought to be punished, whatever else we ought to do about criminal behaviour. The conclusion, for all that has been said so far, can be couched differently, by specifying a distinctive concept of *justified punishment*. Such punishment, we say, is of an offender of whom it is known that he was responsible for his offence. The conclusion of our bit of argument may then be put as this: the concept of a justified punishment applies to nothing and talk which makes use of it is incoherent.

There is in fact no reason to conclude this argument by somewhat obscuring observations on the concept of justified punishment. There is no more reason to conclude the other argument by talk of the distinctive political concept of violence. Some may think that this opinion can be supported by showing that neither the concept of justified punishment nor the given concept of violence is entrenched in ordinary usage or in any other relevant usage. This may be true. A better reason is that the guiding intention of both arguments is not merely to change linguistic usage – supposing such an achievement by itself to be even conceivable – but to contribute to a change in attitude, policy and action. Given this, what might be called the standard form for moral judgement is preferable.

Let us then consider the argument in its direct and overt expression, as set out a moment ago. What we have in the first part is that a man is obliged never to act, except perhaps in certain circumstances, simply because someone has told him to do so. The concern of this nostrum is clearly the moral agent or the good man. A good man, we feel, is one who has the trait among others that he does not act without seeing good reason for doing so. He acts in accordance with some fact of personal responsibility, a fact which is not to be escaped and which he does not attempt to escape. We must, it seems, accept this first item of the argument.

It is thought to follow from this that governments are not justified in claiming a right of obedience from their subjects. They cannot, we are told, have authority. Does this follow? Well, it depends on how the thing is taken. It seems likely that there is *some* right, *some* authority, which we must agree a government cannot have if we accept the first part of the argument. Let us settle clearly what particular authority it is that suits the argument. Let us see what kind of authority it is that a government cannot have if the first part of the argument is accepted. Again, what right of obedience is it that a government cannot have if we accept that every man has an obligation not to act, anyway in most circumstances, on the mere ground that he has been told to do so?

To proceed a bit indirectly, let us imagine someone who does *not* have the specified trait of the good man or the moral agent. Imagine a man who is wholly law-abiding and who says that he lives as he does only because the law so directs him. That, he says, is good enough for him. If we pester him a bit, he will *not* assent to various alternative arguments for his living as he does. He will not accept the account that he lives as he does because that is the lawful way *and* the law expresses his own will. Nor does it matter to him, if it is true, that the law expresses the will of a majority of the members of his society. He will not accept, either, that a justification of his behaviour is that obedience to the law has the recommendation that it avoids greater losses, of whatever kind, than those that may be involved in disobedience. If he did assent to *any* such explanation of his conduct, he would not be the man we want, not a pure case of the obligation of the special kind that we have in mind.

We may suppose, if we want, that our man sometimes thinks there is a good reason for obeying this or that law, a reason other than that it *is* a law. At other times, he thinks there is such a reason for not obeying a law. None of this makes any difference to him. His life, or the part of it with which we are concerned, is governed by the simple fact of his beliefs about legality and illegality. If something is ordered by law, he does it. He is amoral, indeed what we might call the automatic law-abider, or, just conceivably, he is a man of *one* moral principle. It is, simply, that one ought to abide by the law, and absolutely. He has *no* other relevant moral belief. What gives rise to action on his part is the law, and, it must be remembered, this is not to be taken as involving an enthymeme. It is not that obeying the law has this or that further unmentioned recommendation, as people often believe.

It is such a man, and only such a man, who does accord to his government the authority or right to obedience that fits the argument. It is such a man, and only such a man, who accords to his government an authority that runs against the obligation of which Kant speaks. The authority in question, now that it is more explicit, can be seen to be an extremely curious right, not merely to behaviour but to a certain genesis of behaviour. It is a right to unreflective responses or, as one might fairly say, to a certain sort of person.

3. A concession and its importance

There remains a good deal of mystery about our man and the related authority that a government might be claimed to have. One would face great troubles in attempting to give a full characterization of what we can call the *unreflectively obedient man*. He may indeed be a phantasm of the philosophical imagination. In any case, it does seem necessary to agree, and not merely because of Kant's obligation, that it would be wrong for any government to have the authority in question. It is morally mistaken to think that any government could be justified in claiming *this* right of obedience from its subjects. The second step of the argument is certainly all right.

Most important, to pass on to the third step of the argument, we may grant without hesitation that there is one thing that *cannot* be said against the man who sets a bomb. It is that he has violated an obligation deriving from the government's right to his unreflective obedience. More simply, we cannot condemn him for not having been unreflectively or, as might be said, mindlessly or idiotically obedient. We could only condemn him, it seems, if we took to be praiseworthy, or possibly praiseworthy, a different man: the soldier who kills the peasants without reflecting on what he does and *simply because* his officer has given him a command. We certainly do not regard either the automatic soldier, or the soldier with a single moral principle about obeying all commands, as praiseworthy.[4]

One incidental point is worth a moment before we press on. We were given to understand, before we became clearer about the authority in question, that it *could* be possessed by a government in an ideally democratic state. That is, subjects of that state could accord the authority to their government without infringing their Kantian obligation. This is confusion. What is true, rather, is that it is near enough a *logical impossibility* that the subjects of this state infringe their Kantian obligation. This is a state where all subjects consider, vote on, and in fact approve of all legislation. Given that, their obedience to law cannot count as unreflective obedience. The fact that I participate in making the laws, and agree to them, does not make it morally tolerable to obey them unreflectively. On the contrary, unless I am a bizarrely divided personality, my participation makes it a logical impossibility. The confusion of thinking otherwise points to a fact to which we shall come.

Our present position is that we have conceded the force of an argument against a supposed obligation of obedience, and hence against a particular claim about a government's authority. There can be no such obligation on the part of those who contemplate violence, and no such authority on the part of a government which attempts to stop them. What is in question, as we have seen, is an authority of a striking kind. How important, then, is this concession?

It is said that people do in fact persist in assigning to the state precisely the authority which we have conceded that it cannot have. They have the belief, it is said, that the state has a right to what we have called unreflective obedience. Is this so? It seems to me impossible to think so. Does *anyone* believe that the state has *this* right? Does anyone believe the state has the right about whose nature we have become clear? Does anyone half-believe it? There is no point, of course, in supposing they have some *related* belief. A *related* belief might be acceptable and not be open to rejection by way of Kant's conception of the good man. Hence it would not fit the argument we have been considering.

It may be that many people have had, or indeed now have, attitudes to the state which are *consonant* with a demand for unreflective obedience, as understood above. Assuredly the state has been made an object of a kind of superstition, has been perceived as having a religious character or something akin to one, and has been offered something like worship. There is also deference, usually silly. These attitudes owe something to the nature of governments. They make laws, and these are not seen as the giving of advice or the offering of reasons for certain conduct. Laws, it seems, are imperatives. One does not get, in a statute, a lot of reflection on why it ought to be obeyed. Hence, some may suppose, the implicit stand or position of governments is as follows: Do this because our enacted law demands it.

Still, it is pretty clear that these attitudes of veneration fall well short of the belief that the state has a right to unreflective obedience, that a man who sets a bomb is behaving wrongly *because of this alone, that he has had some thoughts about his behaviour*. It is therefore difficult to resist this first substantial conclusion of our reflections: *the argument we have been considering consists in refuting a quite deplorable belief ascribed to the opponents of political violence but unlikely ever to have been contemplated by them.*

There is another matter, perhaps more important. It may be supposed that whether or not anyone has held to the belief, it nonetheless *is* essential or important to an argued opposition to violence. Hence, its failure is crucial. My second substantial conclusion, which I shall support in three ways, is that none of this is correct either. *That the belief is deplorable and refutable is something without further consequences. It is not a belief important to an argued opposition to violence.*

(i) In recognizing one claim about political authority as deplorably mistaken, we do not commit ourselves to any general view about the impossibility of ascribing any authority to the state. We are certainly not committed to thinking that there is *no* sort of authority or right to obedience that the state can have. We are not committed to thinking that there can be *no* arguments against violence which rest on the existence of society and government, and on a claim they make.

The idea that as a result of the given argument we cannot ascribe *any* authority to the state, which would be important, might arise from the supposition that to accord someone a right to something, or to grant someone authority with respect to some matter, *is* to grant an unquestionable power of decision. This is mistaken, as can certainly be shown.

What needs to be pointed out is that there is a notion of authority that is quite different, a notion that is in no way jeopardized by anything conceded so far. It is also clear, and it is what most or many readers will have had in mind at the beginning of this essay. If I think there is a moral argument for complying with most of a government's commands, and I also think that there exist certain kinds of expectation or support, I may with perfect sense talk of the government's right to obedience. The expectation is on the part of the government and society, and is an expectation of obedience to the government's commands. The support, in part, is support for the government in its attempt to enforce obedience to the commands. For the government to have this right is for it to have authority, indeed authority in the most common sense. It is an authority which can be had without its possessor being taken as godlike.

By way of illustration, suppose that I am a democrat in a democracy. I do not think that any policy the government may pass into law ought to be complied with, but I do think, for various reasons, that *some recommendation* attaches to supporting any policy that is passed into law, although there may be things against it. My central idea is that supporting the policy is supporting the system, which I take to be the best system of government. Quite often, I will vote for policy *A* over policy *B* and think it right to do so. However, if *B* wins over *A*, I will conduct myself according to *B*. Further, I will take the view that there are better reasons for complying with *B*, as a law, than *A*, supposing *A* to be against the law.

Thus there is, in my view, a moral argument for obedience to any democratically enacted law. If others take this view and if there then exists the expectation and support mentioned above, it will be perfectly reasonable to talk of the government's right to obedience, the government's authority. This, incidentally, will be perfectly compatible with the belief that for *some A* and *some B*, there would be better reasons for complying with *A*, as a policy against the law, than *B*, supposing it to be the law.

These are perfectly ordinary conceptions of right and authority. It is clear that they need a good deal of attention, that they raise problems of several kinds. Equally clearly, we can anticipate that it in no way follows, from the fact that a government cannot have a right to unreflective obedience, that it cannot have authority at all. Most important, it does not follow that we cannot ever condemn the man who sets a bomb as having done something against the law, something prohibited by the government as a matter of right or authority.

Perhaps to put the point in that way is to obscure it, or to obscure it for some. The point does not have to do, fundamentally, with the propriety of talking precisely of *rights to obedience* and *authority*. We may feel little inclination to engage in such talk. Indeed, it may be thought that it is talk worth avoiding. The important thing is that there remains open the possibility of argument against violence which depends essentially on the existence of law, society and government, whether or not this argument mentions authority or rights. It can be argued, from several premises, that it is right or that there is a moral reason for obeying the law and hence refraining from violence. The fact that talk of rights and authority is in place (since others are likely to agree, and to give support) is of secondary importance.

(ii) A related idea about an important loss that we suffer, when we give up the specified argument against violence, has to do with the history of political theory. It does appear to be an assumption in 'On Violence' that traditional political theory has had as its principal object the establishing of a government's right to unreflective obedience.[5] It is assumed, it seems, that those who have maintained theories of a social contract, or those who have developed democratic theory, have been attempting to establish that each of a state's subjects has that obligation of obedience which is in conflict with the moral rule about having good reason for action. Hence, one may be led to the idea that all of traditional political theory has nothing of value to say against violence, since traditional political theory is argument for unreflective obedience, which is indefensible. An arsenal of argument has been shown to be empty.

However, it is a spectacular unlikelihood that Locke, for example, was concerned to argue for unreflective obedience. He was concerned, rather, *to advance a reason for obedience*. This should not be confused with anything else and, in particular, not with a reason for giving up reflection on the government's commands. It seems that Locke's contention included nothing whatever to which Kant could object. Precisely the same is true of other doctrines of authority which have places in the history of political thought. It does not matter that some of these doctrines come close to demanding *absolute* obedience. In fact, to suppose that the traditional political thinkers were struggling towards a proof of the rightness of *unreflective* obedience is to suppose them pretty well out of touch, or a bit dotty. We must see them as spending a long time giving us reasons for obeying the government, in the hope that we shall forget them.

Scholarship is not required for the main point, however. It is plain that the traditional political doctrines *can* be used in a certain way. Whatever use may have been made of them, they *can* be used to argue for a familiar right of a government to obedience, a right of the kind mentioned a moment ago, something to be sharply distinguished from the right to unreflective obedience. For example, there are the arguments to the effect that a democratic government is superior in several aspects to a dictatorship. One can proceed, in particular, towards the conclusion that there is much to be said against violence, conceived fundamentally as a use of force that has been prohibited.

(iii) There is one other idea that may come to mind in connection with the supposed seriousness of the concession about unreflective obedience. It is perhaps a more natural idea than either of its predecessors. As we have seen, there are a number of arguments which may issue in the conclusion that the state has *an* authority, *a* right to obedience, ordinarily conceived. On many occasions, it may be felt, this conclusion will carry the day over any other consideration. Certainly it will often carry the day over a man's sincere conviction that he ought to do what the state forbids, or ought not to do what the state commands. The state is to override conscience. Some may think that what we have in the end, then, in such cases, is in fact an assertion of the state's right to unreflective obedience. Some may think that claims of the ordinary kind about a right to obedience, despite what has been said, do issue in the indefensible assertion of a right of unreflective obedience.

Fortunately, this is confusion. We may indeed assert that the state may force a man to act, as we say, against his conscience. Sometimes doing so appears to raise moral questions and sometimes it does not. In no case, however, does doing so amount to the securing of unreflective obedience. To be unreflectively obedient is to act, more or less willingly, on the say-so of another. It is to give over one's conscience to another, by not thinking at all or by having one mistaken moral thought. It is *not* a matter of being *compelled* by another, or by the state, to act in a certain way. A man who is being compelled successfully to keep the law is being obedient, but not unreflectively obedient.

Indeed, one might say that if he *is* being compelled, it is logically impossible that he is being unreflectively obedient, since behaviour of the latter kind requires that he obey another *only* because of the other's *command*. To assert that the state may often force a man to act against his conscience, then, which may be the upshot of certain arguments about authority, is *not* to assert that the state ever has a right to unreflective obedience.

In summary of my entire discussion, then, there is a conceivable belief about a government's authority and hence a conceivable condemnation of a man who engages in political violence. It is that he is failing in a particular obligation: to obey the law for the reason, merely, that it has been made. Such a condemnation is deplorable, since it presupposes that the man should be morally irresponsible. The argument against it, set out in three parts above, is conclusive. However, it is entirely doubtful that those who oppose violence have ever attempted the given condemnation. It would be mistaken, further, to suppose that this condemnation of violence enters into other things. It is not relevant to other contentions which mention a government's authority. Its wrongfulness does not cast doubt on traditional claims in political theory, and it does not put in question a belief we have that a man may sometimes be forced by the state to go against his conscience.

4. Principles and propositions

Let us make a fresh start, by considering a fundamental part of Rawls's celebrated book, *A Theory of Justice*. In this part, or these parts, it advances two basic principles for judging or changing societies, and also a number of propositions about political obligation. The argument for the principles is of the same distinctive kind as the arguments for the propositions, and has to do with the idea of a social contract.

However, the basic principles and the propositions about political obligation are connected by more than the fact that they have similar supporting arguments. This is so, as may be guessed, since any claim about political obligation in a society must have a very great deal to do with the acceptability or unacceptability of that society and hence with correct principles for judging societies. It is hardly too much to say that one's political obligation *depends* on the goodness or badness of one's society.

Of course, the appraisal of societies comes into one's reflection on political violence where the special matter of political obligation is not in question. For example, there obviously are arguments against violence which do not have to do with obeying the law but do nonetheless have much to do with the state of societies. One can argue against violence, obviously, by citing the tolerable state of a society, and without mentioning the illegality of violence. Basic principles of judgement thus have a general importance. We shall pay full attention both to the two which are offered here and to the particular argument which is offered for them.

In what follows I shall expound in turn the argument having to do with a social contract, then give the principles, and the propositions about political obligation, and then go on to objections and indeed to what I take to be a refutation. By way of anticipation, one of the two principles has to do with certain traditional liberties and the other with the distribution of socio-economic goods. The propositions have to do with what is called a *natural duty* to obey the law and in general support one's society, and what is called an *obligation* to carry on in much the same way. Violence, given the duty and the obligation, is prohibited, or as good as prohibited.

To begin with what is presented as the fundamental part of the argument before us, we must engage in an activity of imagination. We imagine an assembly of people agreeing on the nature of their coming society. We do not engage in the speculation, rightly dismissed by Hume in his essay on the Social Contract, that they did once exist, or in the bizarre idea that we have inherited obligations from such actual founders of our own societies. We do not suppose, either, that our imagined people in their proceedings serve as a representation of some enterprise of agreement into which we ourselves enter tacitly by living in a society. None of these things is in question here. We merely conceive of people of a certain kind and in a certain situation agreeing on principles which will govern the society of which they are to be members.

It is of the first importance that our imagined people have particular characteristics and not others, and are in a particular situation. (i) They are *self-interested.* (ii) They are *equal* to one another in their freedom to advance conceptions and principles for consideration. (iii) They are *rational.* That they are rational is no more than that they choose the best means to their ends, these ends being the possession of 'primary goods', and that they do not suffer from envy. Lastly, their situation is such that they know or believe certain things, but not others. (iv) They are said to have an awareness of general facts of human psychology, society, politics and economics. (v) It is essential that *none of them, however, knows anything of his own individual future in the society to come.* He does not know what his own natural assets and abilities will be, his economic and social place, even his own psychology or his conception of what is good. He thus does not know if he will be intelligent or otherwise, rich or poor, with or without prestige, black or white, male or female, and so on.

It is argued that our imagined assembly would agree on two principles as the basis of their coming society. They are principles of distribution, usually referred to in a somewhat question-begging way as principles of justice. Despite this good name, as we shall see, exception can be taken to them.

The first is that each member of a society is to have a right to the greatest amount of liberties which is consistent with each other member having the same. The liberties include political rights, freedom of expression, freedom of the person, and the right to hold private property. It is important that the first principle, named the Principle of Liberty, has priority over the second. That is, it is to be acted on first if both cannot be acted on together, and there are to be no departures from it at any stage of a society's development in the interest of a benefit in economic or social goods or their distribution. These latter things are the subject of the second principle.

It, the Principle of Difference, specifies allowable differences between social classes in socio-economic goods. The first part of that principle is that 'social and economic inequalities are to be arranged so that they are . . . to the greatest benefit of the least advantaged . . .'[6] What is intended appears to amount to two conditional propositions. The first is that *if* one class in a society is better off in goods, this must somehow have the effect that the worst-off class in the society is better off than it would be without the inequality. This states a morally necessary condition of an inequality, a necessary condition of the relative positions of the classes. It is a necessary condition of some people being well-off, relatively speaking, that those who are worst-off also benefit. They would be still worse off if the well-off were not exactly as well-off as they are. The second proposition is that if a worst-off class is better off as an effect of another class's being in a better position, the latter class must remain in its fortunate position. This states a morally sufficient condition of the same inequality. It is a sufficient condition of some people being well-off that the worst-off also benefit.

By the first conditional proposition, then, to put the matter another way, we have it that the existence of a better-off class is *permissible* only if something else is true, and by the second proposition we have it that the existence of the better-off class is *obligatory* under the same condition.

As will be seen on reflection, the principle does not by itself tell one what equality or inequality a particular society should have. *No* inequality is allowable which does not improve the lot of the worst-off. Indeed, *if* a departure from a state of *absolute equality* in a particular society were not to make everyone better off, including a worst-off class which would then come into existence, the departure would not be acceptable. On the other hand, *any* inequality in a society is obligatory which *does* improve the lot of a worst-off class. It is therefore a logical possibility that the principle be satisfied in a society of no social and economic inequality whatever, in a society of overwhelming inequality, or in any society in between. The principle leads to a particular society only when it is conjoined with certain special propositions about individuals and their behaviour, resources and so on.

The particular propositions which are assumed in the doctrine before us, and which lie behind the Difference Principle, are to the effect that some inequality will indeed be required in any society if all of its members, including some who have a lesser amount of social and economic goods, are to be as well off as they can be. Any alternative, a system with less or no inequality, will result in everyone, including the individuals just mentioned, being worse off. All this depends on the familiar reasoning that favourable inequalities are *incentives* which are necessary for a higher production of goods.

The Principle of Difference, as I have said, has two parts, of which we now have one before us. In its second part, it is to the effect that all members of the society are to have a considerable and equal opportunity to gain any allowable positions of favourable inequality, say wealth or power. This is not an afterthought, of secondary importance. On the contrary, this second part of the second principle has priority over its first part. The society will not improve the lot of a worst-off class if this can be done only by giving some members an unequal opportunity to secure positions of favourable economic and social inequality.

As for priority generally, then, the Principle of Liberty ranks first. Traditional rights, such as the right to vote, come before progress towards equal opportunity and the reduction of poverty. The second part of the Principle of Difference ranks second. Equal opportunity to become as rich as is permitted, for example, comes before the reduction of the poverty of a worst-off class. The first part of the Difference Principle, having to do with a worst-off class, ranks last.

As I have said, it is argued that our imagined assembly would agree on the two principles and also their priority or ranking, which is evidently of fundamental importance. Let us call this *the basic proposition* of the doctrine before us. It *appears* to be basic, certainly, and it is certainly so regarded by Rawls. It is, to repeat, that the imagined people, people in what is sometimes called *the Original Position*, having the qualities they have and in their prescribed ignorance and belief, would in fact choose the principles and their ranking.

The basic proposition is thought to enter essentially into an argument for the rightness of the two principles, the two principles *as ranked*, which is always to be understood. It is not that this proposition, that the members of the imagined assembly would agree on the principles, is taken to support the conclusion that these would be the correct principles for *their* coming society, which society we can also imagine. The basic proposition is thought to be part of an argument for the moral superiority of the principles for actual societies.[7] *Our own societies* are acceptable to the extent that they are informed by these principles rather than others, and this is a conclusion thought to be supported by the basic proposition. More precisely, the two principles are morally superior within the class of principles which have to do with the amount and distribution of goods. The two principles provide the correct answer to what is named the question of distribution or justice. A society governed by the two principles, to look ahead, will be a society in which political violence will be unjustified.

The other part of the argument for the two principles is that the situation in which they allegedly would be chosen, the Original Position, would be a *fair* one.[8] The conditions under which an agreement on the principles would be reached in the imagined assembly would be fair to all. That is to say or to make the evaluation that no one would be under any disadvantage, or, more explicitly, under any wrongful disadvantage. What is important, and likely to be overlooked, is not that none of them has any disadvantage, where that is to talk simply of matters of fact. Rather, *none of them has any disadvantage of which we disapprove*. A horse-race illustrates the distinction. None of the horses is at a disadvantage, in the sense of wrongful disadvantage, because some of the horses carry more weight and thus, factually speaking, have a disadvantage.

What is important to the argument is that it is the conditions or the circumstance that would be fair, as distinct from the principles chosen, of which the same might be said. The conditions in question are of course those already mentioned, including the ignorance of the members of the imagined assembly as to their individual futures. The conditions secure that members of the assembly would be prevented from discriminating against any group in the society to come.

The whole argument before us, then, is taken to be this:

(i) the proposition that a certain choosing-circumstance would be a fair one,
(ii) the basic proposition, that people in that circumstance would choose the two principles, and
(iii) the conclusion that the two principles are justified.

The conclusion, more fully, is that the ordered principles of Liberty and Difference are those by which we are to assess our own societies. To the extent that these basic principles are realized in it, a society is a morally acceptable one. To the extent that a society is not in accord with the principles, it is not morally acceptable. We shall return to the two principles, and to the given argument for them, after we have before us the related propositions about political obligation.

Any proposition about political obligation, as we have already noticed, depends essentially on the state of society. We might then have in mind, in thinking of political obligation, an imagined society which is *fully in accord* with the two principles we have been considering. This might be of use in developing a theory. We might instead have in mind a society, to describe it quite insufficiently, which *comes near* to realizing the two principles. We might rather have in mind, as in fact we shall, our own societies. It is part of the doctrine we are considering that they have gone some considerable way towards realizing the two principles. In speaking of our societies, I mean such as the societies of Britain and America.[9]

The first proposition is that we, the members of these societies, have a *natural duty*. To express the proposition differently, we ought all to accept that we have a certain natural duty. It has two parts. The first is that we are to comply with, and do our share in, the just or nearly just institutions which are thought already to exist in our societies. A just institution, by specific definition, is one which is in accord with the two principles.

That the institutions are just or nearly just is not the whole argument for the duty. Of course, that the institutions are just or nearly so could naturally be taken on its own as a reason for political obligation. If a society is a good one, then as a matter of logic there is a duty to conform to it and support it, which will principally be a matter of conforming to its law. However, as we shall see in a moment, this reason for political obligation is in fact not all of the argument which is presented.

The natural duty, in its second part, is to assist in the establishing of new arrangements, just or more just, in areas of one's society where they do not yet exist. It is to be noted that the duty, in both its parts, does not derive in any way from our own voluntary acts. It is partly derived, as I have said, from the nature of one's society but not at all from any act, say of promising or of taking benefit, which one has performed.

It will be clear that we do not have a precise account of this duty. In particular, we do not have a precise understanding of its weight. However, we are certainly to understand that the duty is a very considerable one. Certainly it is to be taken as ruling out acts of political violence. It is a part of our duty not to engage in violence, since we must comply with just institutions and it is accepted as part of the doctrine before us that our institutions of law are tolerably just. Indeed, it appears to be accepted in the doctrine that most or almost all of the institutions of our societies are either just or else decently on the way to it. Their being just, to repeat, is for them to be in accord with the two principles.

To come on to the argument for the natural duty, it is made to depend in part on this proposition: that it would be agreed by an imagined assembly of persons, somewhat different from before, that the members of societies like ours ought to have this duty. Those in the assembly, we suppose, are contemplating the possibility of being members of a society like ours. Hence, they have rather more general knowledge of their future society than those people choosing basic principles whom we imagined a little way back.[10] However, our present assembly is in other respects like the first one. The people in it are self-interested, equal, rational, and quite ignorant of what particular position each will have in the society to come. These things make for fairness.

Hence the whole of the argument for our natural duty, as will be expected, is as follows: a certain imaginable assembly would agree on such a duty for the members of societies like ours, more or less just societies, and this would be an agreement made in a fair situation, or under conditions of fairness. The argument, then, is analagous to the one for the two principles. It is pretty clear, incidentally, that an assembly would agree on the duty if, as we may suppose, it would earlier have agreed on the two principles, although under conditions of somewhat greater ignorance, and if our societies are taken to be decently on the way to implementing the two principles.

The second proposition to be considered is that we have a certain *obligation*, which is something distinct from the natural duty, to behave in certain ways. Suppose that by our voluntary actions we have gained benefits from an institution in our society, and furthermore, that the institution is a just or nearly just one. Under these conditions we have an obligation to support or to play a part in the institution in question. Thus we have both a natural duty and an obligation to support certain institutions. It appears that the institution of law counts as one of these. We have an obligation, then, as well as a duty, not to engage in political violence.

The whole argument for our having this obligation is of the same kind again. It is in part that the imagined assembly, contemplating membership in a society like ours, would agree on the obligation. In its other part the argument is that this would be an agreement made in a fair situation, one where no one was under a wrongful disadvantage.

5. The arguments reduced

The first of my objections, which will take a bit of time to lay out, has to do with the family of arguments. What I shall have to say pertains to all of them but I shall speak mainly of the first one, for the two principles of justice. That argument, if the repetition is bearable, is (i) that a certain choosing-circumstance would be a fair one, (ii) that people in that circumstance would choose the two principles, and therefore (iii) that the principles are to be accepted.

This argument consists of an evaluative or normative premise and a factual premise. It is, then, of a familiar kind. The evaluative premise, that a certain situation of choosing would be a fair one, however much we may be inclined to accept it, is in a certain sense unsupported.[11] No proof of it is offered. We thus have an argument of precisely the kind that has led many philosophers and others to say that the evaluative conclusions which are drawn are without 'justification'. Hence, what might be called the first and traditional enterprise of moral philosophy, to attempt to find firm foundations, is in no way advanced by the argument which includes the basic proposition. These are conclusions about the argument for the two principles as we are given it, and as I have just sketched it. In what follows I shall give a more explicit statement of the argument. As will be apparent, the same judgements can be made on the more explicit argument.

Perhaps, however, no justification of the kind traditionally pursued is possible. It may be that in reflection of this kind we have only lesser possibilities, one of which is to begin with the plain assertion of an unproved evaluative premise. It may even be that this is no worse than beginning from unquestioned 'axioms' in other kinds of inquiry. Let us take up this point of view, which cannot be confident but is surely reasonable enough, without further discussion. That is, let us agree to have some evaluative premise or other whose credentials are simply taken to be acceptable.

Both the evaluative and the factual premise get their detail or indeed their identity from the specification of the imagined assembly. It is necessary, at this point, to recall its features. It is (a) an assembly in which each person can and does pursue his own interest. (b) Each person has an equal ability and opportunity to do this. (c) Each makes a rational or effective choice, one which does in fact serve his ends and does not proceed from envy. The latter, envy, is taken to be a willingness to have one's own position worsened in order to worsen the position of another person who is better off. (d) Each is ignorant of any natural capabilities or attributes he will have in the society to come, his attitudes and moral outlook, his wealth or poverty, his social position. He does not know his future race, colour, religion, politics, culture, income or social standing. On the other hand, (e) each person has general beliefs about human psychology and about society, politics and economics. These beliefs are in fact regarded as being true, as being knowledge. It becomes apparent that they are principally beliefs about the paramount importance of liberty in societies and, it seems, the necessity of inequality to general well-being. The latter belief, implied by the Difference Principle, has to do with the familiar doctrine about an incentive system.

The evaluative premise, then, is that an assembly of people satisfying all these conditions, (a) to (e), would constitute a fair choosing-situation, one involving no wrongful disadvantage. However, to come now to a first principal point, it is entirely clear that our acceptance of this premise, assuming that we do accept it, does not come out of thin air. What it comes out of are some moral convictions and some beliefs which we happen to have. As seems plain from a number of passages, Rawls is aware of this fact if he does not state it so plainly or give it the prominence or repetition which he accords to other facts of the theory.[12]

What are the convictions and beliefs? There can be no mystery about that. They are convictions and beliefs which are given expression or effect by the conditions (a) to (e) mentioned above.

We have the conviction (A) that each member of a society, each member of an actual society, has a right to goods, a rightful claim to what is in his interest. We accept (B) that each member has an equal right to such goods, or, at any rate, that we must pay attention to considerations of equality. We accept (C) that steps must be taken to realize each member's right, but that a man should not be worse off simply in order to reduce the benefits of someone else. We accept (D) that the rights in question do not depend on certain things, which are to be regarded as irrelevant. These will include race, colour, religion and so on. That is, we have convictions that certain facts about members of our societies ought to be irrelevant, and these are precisely such facts as those about their futures which the members of the imagined assembly are denied.

If our acceptance that the imagined situation would be fair must come out of these convictions, there is also something else from which it derives. We think, presumably, that the entire speculation is in another way acceptable. A fair choosing-situation, obviously, is one in which the people in question are not misled and do not have false beliefs. They are not disadvantaged in that way. Our acceptance of the imagined situation as fair, then, to put the matter briskly, must derive from (E) beliefs which *we* have about the important place of liberty in societies and also, presumably, about incentive systems.

It is the work of a moment, I think, to put to rest any doubt about the claim that our acceptance of the imagined choosing-situation as fair, assuming we do accept it, does depend on the given convictions and beliefs. Suppose that we did believe some benighted proposition contrary to (A). That is, suppose we believed that some members of societies, somehow identified, do not have any right to goods. If we did believe this, we would *not* approve as fair a choosing-situation of such a kind that it gave rise to a society where *every* member had such a right. Suppose that we believed, contrary to (D), that a man should be paid more simply because he is white-skinned. Suppose that we believed, contrary to (E), that it is just mistaken to give more importance to traditional liberties than to the reduction of poverty. We would then not approve of a choosing-situation which, in a word, does not reflect these beliefs. We would not regard it as a fair one.

The upshot is that the argument we are considering, to make it explicit, consists in:

(i) some moral convictions and some beliefs, which lead us to accept
(ii) that a certain imagined situation for choosing principles would be fair,
(iii) the basic supposition that people in such a situation would choose two principles, and
(iv) the conclusion that the principles have a recommendation.

We can call this the *Contract Argument* for the principles.

Some may be inclined to think, at first thought, that the first premise is not logically distinct from the second. The truth is otherwise. One part of the second premise, about fairness, is to the effect that a choosing-situation in which people could not allow the colour of a man's skin to determine his liberties would be in that respect fair. This is evidently distinct from the conviction that a man's skin-colour ought to be irrelevant to his liberties.

Some may think, secondly, that to set out the argument in the four steps is to set it out uneconomically. They may feel that it can be set out more efficiently as it was before, in the last section, consisting just in the assertion that a certain choosing-situation would be a fair one, the assertion that people in that situation would choose the two principles, and the conclusion that the principles have a recommendation.

Several things might be pointed out about this. The most important is that what appears in the first part of the four-part argument must in fact occur in any expression of the argument which is complete. It is plain enough where it does occur in the three-part argument. It is bundled into the initial premise, that a certain choosing-situation would be a fair one, one in which no one is at a wrongful disadvantage. To assert this premise, plainly, is partly to assert that the choosing-situation is in accord with certain convictions. The situation, for example, is in accord with the conviction that skin-colour ought to be irrelevant to certain things.

In what follows, then, let us have in mind the four-part form of the Contract Argument. What is to be said for this form, in general, is simply that it is fully explicit. All that I shall have to say of the argument in this form, evidently, will be relevant to other forms of it.

Let us put all this aside for a moment and consider a different and common kind of reflection on societies and principles. Suppose one wishes to arrive at principles for the governance of one's actual society. One wishes, that is, to get an answer to the question of distribution or justice. One begins with one's convictions and beliefs. They are to the effect that each member of a society is to be regarded as having a right to goods of one kind and another, and that steps are to be taken to secure this right. As it happens, one's convictions and beliefs are precisely those sketched a little way back, (A) to (E). *Having got them straight, one advances directly to the conclusion that the best answer to the question of justice amounts to the two principles of justice of which we know.* The principles, of course, as in the case of the Contract Argument, are in good part no more than *generalizations* or *summations* of the convictions, although there is much more that might be said. What one will have done is produce what we shall call an *Ordinary Argument* for the two principles.

The first thing that I wish to point out about the two arguments is that the Ordinary Argument is *as good* as the Contract Argument in giving support to the two principles.

From what has been said so far, of course, it is less than clear that either argument is much good. There is an impressive gap, or rather, nothing so clear as a gap, between the premise or the premise-set and the shared conclusion. This summing-up is not just adding. It is arguable, of course, that many principles could not get support from either the single premise of the Ordinary Argument or the set of three premises in the Contract Argument. Racist principles, and principles of discrimination generally, are in this group. However, there are more left over than only the Principles of Liberty and Difference.

Can the Contract Argument be improved? In *A Theory of Justice* a good deal of effort is put into arguing for the truth of the basic proposition: that the assembly would choose the two principles. The argument, in one important part, is that each member of the assembly, in comparing different principles or groups of principles, would realize that all of them, save total equality, would have within them the possibility of different upshots for the member in his future life in the society. He might be among the rich or among the poor, for example, and he cannot know in advance. He would, it is suggested, be of such attitudes as to *maximin*: that is, to choose the particular conception whose worst possible upshot for him would be more acceptable than the worst possible upshots of other conceptions. Each member of the assembly would, as a result, be led to favour the Principle of Difference. What this amounts to is in fact a further characterization of the assembly.

There is another essential matter to be kept in mind if we proceed in this way, giving a further characterization of the assembly. We must also suppose, to keep the whole doctrine standing, that the enlarged conception *persists* as a conception of a *fair* choosing-situation. *We* must then have certain convictions or beliefs. We must, in short, have a commitment to the maximum principle. We must feel it is a good idea to play safe.

I have suggested that at first sight, or in its first presentation, the Contract Argument is no better than the Ordinary Argument in producing the two principles of justice as conclusion. We now suppose, however, that the Contract Argument can be strengthened. This is done by characterizing the imagined assembly more fully and adding the feature just mentioned. If the Contract Argument can be strengthened in this way, however, to come to the main point here, it is necessarily true that the Ordinary Argument can be strengthened to the same extent. One adds one's strengthening conviction to the premise of the Ordinary Argument. One adds the conviction that one should always choose the policy whose worst upshot will be best. In general, *whatever* is done to the Contract Argument can have a counterpart with respect to the Ordinary Argument. The latter will be as good, bad or indifferent as the former.[13]

What follows from this, I take it, is the conclusion that the *actual grounds* implicit in the Contract Argument, however adumbrated, are identical with the grounds in some version of the Ordinary Argument. *All* that actually gives support to the conclusion in the Contract Argument is the first premise, a certain collection of convictions and beliefs. All that actually gives support to the conclusion is exactly and no more than that which supports the conclusion in the Ordinary Argument. *What we have called the basic proposition in the Contract Argument is logically irrelevant to it. So too is the evaluative proposition that the imagined choosing-situation would be a fair one.* The Contract Argument is the Ordinary Argument with two superfluous parts. What is taken to be the foundation of the Contract Argument is in fact no part of the structure. Reflection on the basic proposition, so-called, let alone prolonged reflection, is idle. So too for the proposition about fairness.

(The analogy is incomplete and maybe a bit unfair, but one is put in mind of the sanguine sociologist, say, who comes to some conclusion about the nature of society. He does so only on the basis of certain *evidence* and by way of certain *canons of inquiry*. He proceeds to attribute belief in precisely his evidence as well as acceptance of precisely his canons of inquiry to an imagined conference of sociologists. He is pleased to discover, and entirely right to discover, that the conference would confirm his conclusion. Someone will have to point out that from the point of view of the logic of the situation, the validity of the argument, the imagined conference is an irrelevancy.

The analogy between our contracting assembly and the sociological conference, incidentally, becomes nearer to complete if we make our sociologist a bit odder still. He imagines a conference of sociologists who do not in fact have precisely his evidence and canons, but, for some reason, draw a conclusion *as if they had*. What leads me to say this, of course, is that the members of the assembly have no moral convictions, but, for reasons we know, they behave as they would if they did have.)

It is worth noticing, in partial explanation of the error of thinking that the basic proposition does have some logical utility, that something like it does have utility when it turns up in other speculations about a Social Contract, those traditional ones mentioned some way back in this essay and having to do with actual people and the grounds of political obligation. Suppose that somehow *we do tacitly commit ourselves* to our societies and their principles. We may, then and afterwards, have convictions that lead us to think the principles are good ones. Thus there is that reason for going along with them. However, our observance of the principles also has this to be said for it: we promised it. This proposition, one that is related to the basic proposition in the doctrine we are considering, provides an independent argument of some strength or other for our observance. At any rate the proposition will do so if it is true.

I should like to anticipate one objection to what has been claimed. The people in the imagined assembly, we have granted, would *agree* on the principles. This is part of the Contract Argument but not the Ordinary Argument. The objection, which will barely survive being made explicit, is that some recommendation is shown to attach to the principles by the fact that they would be *agreed upon* by the people.

What recommendation is it? We must not drift into thinking, obviously, that any real person has ever made such an agreement and so acquired an obligation. The Social Contract, in its traditional form, is not our subject. It does not matter if we grant, as we are urged, that *'we' would* agree to the principles *if* we were as the people in the Original Position are.[14] *We* are different, have never been there, and have made no agreement.

If we stick firmly to the supposition, that imagined people would agree on the principles, there is still no recommendation in the bare fact of their agreement. To see this, suppose we imagine an assembly made up of people who know that the coming society will have in it weak and powerful members. Moreover, and more important, each person in the assembly knows where he will turn up, whether he will be weak or powerful. Suppose, then, that the assembly comes to agree on principles which will favour those who will be powerful, and that this comes about essentially as a result of an awareness of that future state of affairs. We will not suppose that the fact that there would be this agreement would recommend the principles. The mere fact of agreement in an imagined assembly is by itself of no relevance to us. If, incidentally, the example just imagined is taken not to be one of satisfactory or full agreement, but rather an example involving something like coercion, it is easy enough to think of an alternative. There is the assembly with false beliefs, to mention but one.

We thus have the conclusion that what confers relevance, if no more, on an imagined agreement, are the conditions under which it is made. The recommendation of the agreed principles, in that case, rests on the conditions, and then on the convictions that support them. What we have is the Contract Agreement as sketched, with no reliance placed on the bare fact of agreement.

In any case, talk of agreement in the imagined assembly, like talk of *an assembly* at all, is quite otiose for a reason so far unmentioned. What we are contemplating, if we are following the instructions, is an assembly of *identical persons*. At any rate we contemplate them only insofar as they are identical. Each is taken only to have precisely the qualities that have been mentioned. If we set about assigning them other qualities, perhaps various and compensating knowledges of capabilities of judgement, we depart from our instructions. It is not suggested that we are to do this, and if we attempt it, the truth of the basic proposition becomes still more uncertain than it is if we follow our instructions. What we do, then, in short, is imagine identical persons. In this case, all talk of *agreement* is otiose or pointless. We might as well have imagined *a single individual* and not an assembly.[15] For this reason alone, an elaborated theory of the kind we are considering verges on the ridiculous.[16]

So much for the structure of the Contract Argument for the two principles. Perhaps, in the confines of this essay, I have attended too much to the structure of the argument. Still, the doctrine about political obligation we are considering is given to us as all of a piece, a piece in which the Contract Argument is fundamental.

Also, there is the larger matter already noticed, having to do with The Impressive in political philosophy. It is worth remarking, in this connection, that it is not as if the structure of the argument were something in every way distinct from the force of the argument, the final worth. Strictly speaking, of course, the final worth of the argument is not affected by the discovery that the structure has redundant parts, parts on which the conclusion does not depend. Nonetheless many people are likely to think more of the Contract Argument when it is presented to them than they would think of the Ordinary Argument. The structure itself distracts attention from the prime question of whether the two principles are an adequate generalization and reconciliation of the collection of attitudes and beliefs. One is less likely to see how much a matter of hesitant judgement it must be, rather than a matter of anything like plain logical fact, that the two principles follow as a conclusion from what goes before. One is less likely to see, too, how hesitant one's judgement must be about supposed consequences of the principles, notably those having to do with violence.

To persist with structure for a moment more, there are also the given arguments for the two propositions about political obligation. Again, what is taken to be fundamental is logically irrelevant. There are certain special complexities here but let us pass them by. What I shall do is merely state, pretty roughly, the actual arguments which are contained in the presented arguments. These actual arguments are analogous, of course, to the Ordinary Argument.

(a) Given certain convictions and beliefs, the same as outlined above for the Ordinary Argument, and given the belief that our societies are decently on the way towards achieving a goal defined by the two principles of justice, it follows that we have a natural duty to support and advance the institutions of our societies. In particular we must abide by the law and refrain from violence.

(b) Given the convictions and beliefs as before, and given that we have chosen to benefit from institutions in our societies which are in accord with the two principles, we have an obligation to play our part in the institutions. In particular, we are obliged to abide by the law and refrain from violence.

6. The principles again

It seems plain enough that the Ordinary Argument does not come near to *establishing* the two principles in their ordering as the basic principles for the judging and directing of societies. It follows, given what has been said, and perhaps it is evident anyway, that the same is true of the Contract Argument. It may be, further, that nothing so neat and ordered as is suggested by the word 'argument', as usually used, will ever convince one that any basic principles are the right ones. Also, a ramified thing which is larger and looser than an argument, if it does produce a kind of conviction about particular principles, is unlikely to 'establish' them, let alone 'demonstrate' them. It is unrealistic to hope for the neat cogency which the words suggest.

It must be allowed, of course, despite the weakness of the Ordinary Argument and the Contract Argument, that their supposed conclusion is nonetheless correct. That is, it might be that the two principles are indeed the right principles for society. Are they? The question is obviously too large to be settled finally here. Something needs to be said, however, partly because of the relation of the two principles to the propositions about duty and obligation, propositions on which we also need to come to some judgement. They also may be better, so to speak, than the given argument for them.

The two principles are mainly compared by Rawls with the Principle of Utility. The latter principle is taken to be the most important alternative, and much argument against it is offered. The argument in the end is fully familiar: the Principle of Utility countenances inequality or unfairness, indeed calls for it, when this happens to maximize the total of satisfaction or minimize the total of dissatisfaction. The two principles are likely to be regarded as superior to the Principle of Utility in that they are in several obvious ways concerned with equality. The first principle calls for a certain equality in liberties, that particular equality in which everyone has the greatest possible amount of them. The second principle is concerned to improve the lot of the worst off in terms of socio-economic goods by allowing certain inequalities in terms of such goods. The two principles are like the Principle of Utility, of course, in being consequentialist: they judge practices, institutions and so on by their consequences. Or, to be more precise about the nature of consequentialism, they judge things in terms of their consequences in felt experience, as distinct for example from such so-called consequences as *the right thing's having been done*.

To grant that the two principles are superior to the Principle of Utility, however, is not to grant all that much. There are other principles which also are superior to Utility. These also have the virtue of giving a place to equality. The one which seems to me right will be suggested by certain criticisms that can be made of the two principles.

(i) By the first principle, that of Liberty, a society is to accord to its members the maximum amount of liberties consistent with all members having the same amount. This principle takes precedence over the second one, the Principle of Difference. Let us consider this precedence, if briefly. It is, in part, that there is to be no infringement of a man's or a group's liberties even if this will serve to raise the socio-economic level of the worst-off class in society. There is this prohibition on interference with liberties at any stage of social progress.

It is not made at all clear what we are to have in mind as the liberties in question. This remarkable failure makes discussion disagreeable, but not impossible. If a rough description is worthwhile, let us think of those things, including various property-rights, which are commonly mentioned as liberties in our societies. Surely it cannot be acceptable that there should be an *absolute* prohibition on interference with these things. It is not too much to say that social progress in the past, now approved by all, has *depended* on infringements of such things. Can it be thought that no possible future advancement will be worth an infringement? Is it certain that the present amount of liberties had by each member of our societies is correct? It is nothing like certain. With less of certain liberties, presumably, there would be less socio-economic inequality of the kind which does not help the worst-off. There would be less distress.

There is also an objection which has to do with the fact that the liberties are merely rights in a certain standard sense. That is, to have a liberty is not necessarily to have the power to act on it. My right to hold property does not ensure that I own anything whatever. Should we not focus upon powers? Rawls has something to say of the question but hardly enough. My main criticism here, however, is the other one. The place which should be given to *some* principle about liberties is not the large place given the Principle of Liberty in the doctrine before us.

(ii) There is evidently something, indeed a good deal, to be said for this first part of the Principle of Difference, about necessary inequalities in socio-economic goods. Still, there is a large question to be asked about it. Is it an *effective* socio-economic principle? That is, in the main, is it in such a form as to be most likely to forward its end? It is given as this: A society can and must have all the inequalities of whatever size, if only those, which are necessary to make the position of the socio-economically worst-off better than it would otherwise be. Because of what it strongly implies, this proposal as it stands might reasonably be called defeatist and can undoubtedly be called cautious. Although in its concern for the worst-off it derives from a commitment to equality, it is so expressed as to bring into prominence the declaimed need for incentive inequalities. It thus may encourage those who in fact favour socio-economic inequality that is against the interests of the worst-off. The analogy is a loose one, but it is as if the Utilitarians, instead of urging us to maximize total satisfaction, had urged us to pursue the distress, if only the distress, that will serve to maximize satisfaction in the end. Keep on the look-out for useful unhappiness!

It will be said that caution about ending inequalities is required, and that it is a good thing to give it expression in the formulation of the principle. A single sentence cannot despatch this dispute, but it is worth nothing that socio-economic history shows no shortage of claims, now falsified, about the necessity of various inequalities. There is a related point. Despite history, there is hardly a more established controversy in economic and political thinking than the one between those who believe in the necessity of much inequality as a means to a good end, and those who believe that much less would suffice, or suffice for a better end. On the other hand, there can be little controversy about the proposal that we should pursue an ideal of equality having to do with the least well-off. If we have an area of agreement, or something like it, and an area of controversy, it is as well to separate them. The Principle of Difference brings together what is best kept apart.

It would be mistaken to take this reflection about effectiveness less seriously because it consists in an objection to the emphasis or style rather than just the propositional content of the Difference Principle. One and the same proposition, in a certain sense, can obviously have several different attitudinal embodiments, and hence enter into what it is not silly to count as different principles. What one has in a principle is not only what it states, in some restricted and very literal sense, but also an informing spirit. It is important that what is literally specified by a principle reflects our convictions, but it is quite as important that its style and spirit does so.

(iii) There is also the second part of the Principle of Difference. Should all members of society have an equal opportunity to gain any allowable positions of favourable inequality in socio-economic goods? The question becomes more clearly troublesome when it is put this way: Should all members of society, whatever their natural strengths and weaknesses, have *only* an equal opportunity to benefit from the society's resources? The question needs to be answered by way of the reflection that some individuals must have greater shares of things if they are to avoid distresses which other individuals can easily avoid without having such shares.

(iv) All of the three points made so far about the principles of

Liberty and Difference point towards a more general and fundamental principle. Liberty, it was said, can hardly be allowed to obstruct progress in alleviating distress. What we must have, it was then said, is an *effective* socio-economic principle for the aid of the worst-off. Thirdly, certain kinds of favourable inequality of opportunity are needed by some individuals if they are to avoid certain levels of experience.

The more fundamental and general principle is the Principle of Equality. Briefly expressed, it is that we are to improve the lives of those who are badly off, those at the bottom in terms of distress and satisfaction. We are to work for the well-being of everyone, without exception. It is this principle which must be the foundation of moral, social and political reflection, and it needs to be explicit.

We may think, first, of helping the badly off by means and methods which do not affect at all the well-being of the rest. If the pie of well-being can be enlarged, and the shares of the better-off not lessened, then obviously this is what is to be done. We must act if we can on the familiar exhortation to 'level up' rather than 'level down'. But can we possibly rely on this approach? Is it at all realistic to suppose that we can *sufficiently* increase material and other means to well-being in this way? Very obviously it is not. No one will want to ignore chances of simply increasing the means, but it cannot possibly be that we can be satisfied with this approach. What we must mainly consider is the transferring of means of well-being from some to others.

It is important to be clear about the end or goal of the Principle of Equality. Despite misunderstanding produced by judgements of the kind just made about transferring goods, and despite a certain amount of propaganda and self-deception, the end of the principle is not the reducing of the well-being of the better-off. That *may* happen, certainly, although the likely extent is difficult to judge. The connection between well-being and what we have called the means to it is far from simple. It would be entirely consistent with the true spirit of Equalitarianism to rely entirely on 'levelling up' if that were realistic. To act principally on the other policy, that of transferring goods, since that is essential for the relief of the badly off, is to be moved by a high ideal rather than a base impulse. There is a related truth when the active parties are the would-be beneficiaries. There is no question, of course, of the better-off being reduced to a level lower than that of the hitherto badly off.

A second and related point is that the end of the Principle of Equality is not that of changing the relative positions of the badly off and the better-off. It is not to get people *on a level*, some level or other. It is not, strictly speaking, to reduce inequality. This remains true despite the fact that a foreseeable effect of helping the badly off will be a movement towards equality of well-being with the hitherto better-off. Also, there is the equalizing effect of transferring goods. The end is nonetheless not to produce or to approximate to an equality, but to improve the lot of the badly off.

Since the Principle of Equality is not aimed at worsening the position of the better-off, and, still more relevantly, is not aimed at securing a relationship of equality between all parties, is the principle wrongly named?

In explanation of how it has come about that this principle has got the given name, one important fact is the predictable effect of pursuing the given end. The effect is a tendency towards equality in goods and some tendency towards an equality in well-being. Can it be said, secondly, that the principle has got the given name from the *means* to its end? Well, it is not at all true that the means to the end of helping the badly off *is* a tendency towards equalization in well-being. The great means is the transfer of goods to the badly off. The fact that something like equalization in goods is so intimately bound up with this means has no doubt contributed to the principle's having the name of the Principle of Equality. A third point is that in many circumstances, of which this is one, the means to an end can itself take on a good deal of the character of an end. Typically this is true when there is a struggle to achieve a means to an end. Some may wish to maintain, finally, that the principle has its name because its supporters have generally fallen into confusion, or into envy, and hence have been pursuing equality as their only end. No doubt the mistake has been made by some of them. It is nowhere near true that the true end of the principle has been generally forgotten.

This explanation suggests ground enough for persisting with a traditional name. (There is certainly *no* ground for maintaining that it can reasonably be attached only to a principle whose only aim is that all people be at some same level.) If more defence is needed for speaking of the Principle of Equality, there is one consideration of practical importance. To speak instead of 'The Principle of Concern' or 'The Principle of Benevolence' or 'The Principle of Compensation' would be to fail to direct attention to the only effective means to the end in question, the means of greater equalization in goods. Perhaps there is no other large part of human life where there is so strong an inclination to see the end but to avoid the means.

7. The duty and the obligation

Just as the Contract Argument for the two principles reduces to the Ordinary Argument, so the subsequent arguments about political obligation and hence violence reduce to analogues of the Ordinary Argument. The first of these in one formulation is that given certain convictions and beliefs, and given that our societies are decently on the way to realizing the two principles, it follows that we have a natural duty to support and advance the institutions of our societies. We have a natural duty to obey the law and to refrain from violence.

We may suppose that the conclusion follows from the premises but, as what has been said already clearly suggests, the premises are open to question. The collection of convictions and beliefs is in part at least controversial. For example, there is the belief that certain liberties have an importance greater than anything else. This point was to be anticipated, of course, since the same objection has been made to the summation of the convictions and beliefs in the two principles.

Furthermore, even if we accepted the convictions and beliefs and the two principles without hesitation, there is the question of how far our societies do in fact realize them. Let us give some attention to this, or rather, to the limited question of whether our societies are decently on the way to realizing the Principle of Difference, which, despite what has been said against it, is superior to many other socio-economic principles. That our societies *are* decently on the way to realizing the principle is obviously essential to the argument about duty.

To speak particularly of Britain and America, are these societies tolerably well on the way to having only those inequalities which are consistent with the Principle of Liberty and are necessary if a worst-off class is to be better off than otherwise it would be? The question is far from precise. Let us take it to be tantamount to something else, perhaps slightly better: Are these societies *so much* on the way to having only the specified inequalities that their members have a weighty duty, however 'natural' or 'unnatural', to obey the law? It is allowed, in the doctrine we are considering, that things may *seem* otherwise. That is, it is allowed that it may *seem* likely that there is an awful lot of unnecessary inequality. At this point, an additional economic consideration is introduced.[17]

It is that the production of goods depends not only on an incentive system, but on something that in our societies is closely connected with it, real capital accumulation. What we are to understand is that we could, for one or a few generations, reduce the gap between rich and poor, by reducing benefits to the rich, and that we would not pay the price of reducing the state of life of the poorest. However, this would have the effect of reducing real capital accumulation and hence, in the end, the effect of depriving future generations of the poorest of a certain degree of well-being that might otherwise have been theirs. I have stated the argument briefly but not, I hope, unfairly.

One reply, which seems obvious, is that there is only a contingent connection between real capital accumulation and the existence, as we know it, of extreme economic and social inequality. One can hardly ignore the fact that there exist different economies which satisfy an analogous requirement of real capital accumulation and do not do so by lodging the capital with a class of overwhelming privilege. There seems no quick or slow argument to the conclusion that a society *must* do its saving by sustaining the existence of great inequalities. We need not dismay ourselves by the reflection that the economic theory in question is extensive and unsettled. We can rest on the fact that there do exist economies which face futures as secure as those of America and Britain and do not sustain similar systems of inequality. There *are* economies, as satisfactory as ours, which are without the rich.

Two other things are to be said against the idea, which, it will be as well to say, appears to me a *wild* idea, that our societies are so far on the way to having only the necessary inequalities that it follows that we have a weighty political obligation. It may well be that there exists some such obligation, of course, somehow grounded. What seems absolutely implausible is that it can be grounded on the proposition about necessary inequalities.

The first point is that to think that we *are* decently on the way to having only necessary inequalities is very likely to be out of touch, for one reason or another, with the magnitude of existing inequalities. This is a matter, in part, of that ignorance of the facts of inequality noticed in the first essay in this book. To approach the question of magnitude in one way, it is in no way rhetorical to observe that some large minority of members of our societies, if their lives were altered in a certain way, would experience them as lives of horror. I have in mind an alteration such that their new existence would be one which *is* in fact the lot of another minority now. If we in the minority of privilege bring to mind, and not for a passing moment, what touches us most closely, perhaps our children and their situation, it must be impossible to think of tolerating the alteration. By way of one example, it includes those existing schools which make our commitment to proper opportunity no more than hypocrisy. They are schools which blight and constrict the entire lives of the children who go to them.

Shall we say that such an existence would carry a distress for us unlike the distress now caused to those who now experience it? No doubt this is in some degree true. Distress in part is a consequence of expectation. Destructive circumstances have a lesser effect on those who have not anticipated anything else. For such reasons there once was, in terms of satisfaction and distress, the possibility of a certain defence of the institution of slavery. (Certainly neither the bare lack of such goods as money and property, nor inequality in them, is *by itself* of importance. What is important is avoidance of the experience of distress, and it *may be* avoided despite the absence of certain goods. What matters is well-being, which a person might possess despite inequality of some goods.) Certainly the argument of different expectations is a vanishing one. Each slave-class took up, to an increasing extent, the expectations of its masters. Today, oppressed classes in our societies are aware of their situation to a very considerable degree. Their awareness is not yet ours, but that does not make it reasonable to continue to weigh the goods of the world in two sets of scales. Experienced deprivation in our societies is in fact great.

The other remark about necessary inequalities has already been made in another connection. It cannot be in dispute that virtually every major economic and social advance in history, every advance in the direction of equal well-being, has been resisted by an argument about supposedly necessary inequalities. Almost no one takes the view, now, that the inequalities *were* necessary to things of importance. No one takes the view that any losses suffered did outweigh the gains. What we have here, to speak quickly, is an iron inductive argument in favour of scepticism about all claims as to necessary inequalities in our present societies.

What remains is only to draw a conclusion about the argument for our supposed natural duty to obey the law and hence to refrain from violence. It cannot be that we have no duty whatever. We have *more* of a duty than we would have in a slave-society. It has not been shown, however, to state the proposition as best one can, that there is *a weighty duty*. Our circumstance is *far* from an imagined one, also considered by Rawls, where the members of a society are members of an ideal society and so have a weighty and indeed an overwhelming duty to support it.

Let us leave the duty and pass on to the separate obligation which we are thought to have. Given the same convictions and beliefs as before, and given that we have voluntarily acted so as to benefit from institutions in our societies which are in accord with the two principles, we have an obligation to play our part in the institutions. What is to be said against this is partly the same as with the natural duty. The convictions and beliefs are not beyond question. The two principles are not beyond question. Hence even if the institutions of our societies are in accord with the principles, we do not have the simple fact that we have benefited from institutions which are clearly defensible.

We may reflect, however, that there is *something* to be said for, say, the Principle of Difference. Do we then have a resulting weighty obligation? The answer depends, as before, on whether institutions of our society do in fact come near enough to being in accord with the principle, and hence having only certain necessary inequalities. I have already suggested that there is no reason for thinking so. It is a dream.

There are further difficulties about the obligation. It is not clear, despite what is said about voluntarily accepting benefits, how the obligation is supposed to come into being. Suppose a man does accept a benefit by invoking the law in order to protect his own property, and then breaks a law for political reasons. In so doing he destroys the property of someone else. In what does the wrongfulness of his act consist? What is the particular wrongfulness which has to do with the fact that he has used the law in his own interest previously? Is it that a consideration of consistency or equality enters into the argument? That is, does the wrongfulness consist in treating identical or similar cases, cases of property-ownership, differently? One of the difficulties in the way of this line of argument is that the two cases, although alike when considered in terms of property ownership, are fundamentally different. To say no more, one is a case of *political* violence.

Alternatively, if it is an alternative, does the wrongfulness of the political act consist in the fact that it is not an acceptance of rightful *debt*? This is suggested by the emphasis on voluntary action in connection with the obligation. Here we have it that by voluntarily benefiting from an institution of his society, the man acquires a certain debt. We can say that certain behaviour on his part is now owed, or called for, or fitting. This behaviour is precisely other than the behaviour of destroying the property of others.

There clearly are replies. First, if the man believed that a minority of his society was being degraded, he rightly might not allow himself to be restrained from violent political action by the single fact that he had been a beneficiary himself. Rather the contrary, perhaps.

What is said in explanation and defence of the obligation leaves out of consideration all people other than the man himself and those individuals whose property he may destroy.

Again, assuming that the man does in fact acquire some debt by making use of the law in his own interest, how large is that debt? Could it be that if it exists at all, it is very small indeed? Consider an opposite case. Most people would not feel that a man had gone any way towards justifying the setting of a bomb if he established that he had eschewed, as far as he could, the benefits offered to him by society. He would not do himself much good by pointing out that he had not called the police when his house was broken into. The smallness of his defence indicates the smallness of the accusation that can be made in our primary case, where a man is claimed to have disregarded the debt acquired by voluntarily acting in such a way as to benefit from society.

Our supposed obligation, then, seems a still smaller thing than our natural duty. There *may* be stronger arguments against political violence which are based on a fact of political obligation, and indeed we shall return again to the question.[18] The present argument is no winner.

Let us finish by recalling the main conclusions of this discussion of *A Theory of Justice*.

The Contract Argument for the Principles of Liberty and Difference as ordered, by which we are to judge our societies, contains parts thought to be basic but which in fact contribute nothing to the force of the argument. The same is true of the analogous arguments for our supposed natural duty and our obligation to obey the law, and hence to refrain from violence. There is a likelihood, in the case of each argument, that its expendable machinery will distract attention from its value. Its value is no greater than that of a related ordinary argument.

If one looks at the two principles directly, or, much the same, looks at the conviction and beliefs which are their source, one finds several grounds for objection. One has to do with the place given to liberties, another with the character of the Principle of Difference. The Principle of Equality is needed.

Objection must also be made to the claims about natural duty and obligation. One large point here is that the arguments for the duty and the obligation, and hence for refraining from violence, presuppose that our societies are decently on the way to realizing the Principle of Difference. They are not. They are nowhere near it.

4 ON DEMOCRATIC VIOLENCE

If we look at contemporary writing on political violence in the hope of finding cogent arguments, either for or against it, and if we are not too disposed to take a side, we are unlikely to be satisfied. This pessimism certainly does not derive only from the several pieces of writing looked at in the earlier essays of this book. In Sartre and Fanon, an impassioned commitment to the oppressed issues in the judgement that violence is not only permissible but obligatory. That some men are made less than men, that they have their stature taken from them, appears to be taken as an adequate ground for their violence, violence which is to change them. '... to shoot down a European', we are told, 'is to kill two birds with one stone, to destroy an oppressor and the man he oppresses at the same time.'[1] It is not hard to find questions about the argument, even given some understanding and not merely an awareness of facts about colonial oppression and personality. Most of us, to pass on to but one other example, will be as reluctant to suppose that the 'historical calculus' offered to us by Marcuse can be shown to issue in the conclusion that political violence of the Left generally has a justification.[2] Can there be much more than metaphor in talk of the *rules* given us by history?

Some, of course, will find scepticism about Sartre, Fanon and Marcuse congenial, but not scepticism about others. It is, for me, difficult to see this as other than a result of being too disposed to take a side. To return for a moment to Rawls, we should be as reluctant to take up his equally resolute conclusions.[3] It really cannot be that it is economic *necessity* that principally explains the fact that our societies are still subject to wide and destructive inequalities.

It cannot be that the intransigence of privileged classes is not a principal part of the explanation. If so, we must at least question his prohibition on violence, based largely on the idea that our societies come about as close to decency as can be fairly asked.

It remains obscure what total of things would enter into really effective argumentation, if it is possible, either for or against violence. Certainly some group of basic principles would be fundamental, as would the facts of inequality and the facts of violence. Presumably some complete assessment of claims about political obligation would have a place. There could be no avoiding judgements about replies to violence, reactions justified or unjustified, on the part of the state, privileged classes, and others, and, more generally, there could be no avoiding judgements on the rationality of engaging in violence.

There is also something else, which cuts across some of these subjects. It will be valuable, and I suspect essential, in any effective argumentation, to consider how violence is related to other practices, relevant practices about which we have clearer judgements. One of these, perhaps the most important, is democracy.

Many of those who condemn violence do so on the ground that it is undemocratic. Many of its apologists are in some agreement with those who condemn it. Their endeavour is to find higher reasons for what they accept, implicitly or explicitly, to be undemocratic. My first purposes in this essay are to see clearly how political violence stands to the practice and the rules of democracy, and to the arguments for the practice and the rules. The latter relationship, between some violence and the arguments for democracy, will then enter into a characterization of one important type of political violence. In the end, we shall be further on the way to having an adequately reasoned conclusion about the morality of violence

1. Democracy

We must first recollect and perhaps become clearer about the nature of democracy, or rather democracy as best conceived in the last few decades of the tradition with which most of us are familiar. It is *a practice in which the people choose and then influence those who do govern the nation and direct its relations of war and peace*. This is but a rubric, and a rubric that might stand at the head of different texts. Even so, since we shall be concerned with such systems of government as those in Britain and America, it provides us with a conception which is more apposite than certain alternatives. I have in mind the alternative idea of government *by* the people, and the alternative idea of government whose covert function is the oppression of most of the people by an ascendant class.

We can clarify our conception of democracy by prising apart three groups of features, which also will serve as criteria for the assessment of existing systems. None of this will be amazingly novel stuff, for good reason. Also, while we shall fill out the conception, insofar as it can be done very quickly, we shall certainly not arrive at as precise a conception as might be required in other endeavours than our own. There is no way of setting out the criteria, incidentally, which will bring together in a particular group all and only those criteria that may be seen as alike from *all* reasonable standpoints. In what follows, those that are alike from a standpoint other than mine may turn up in different groups.[4] It is also to be noted that a criterion, in the intended sense, may be more or less satisfied by an existent system of government, or, we may say, not satisfied at all.

(i) *Uncoerced choosing and influencing*. In the practice of democracy, to begin with certain considerations relating particularly to *pre-election* periods, the politics of the electors are not forced upon them. That is to say, roughly, that their attitudes, wants, demands and choices, both interested and in a way disinterested, are of their own making. It cannot be, certainly, that in its politics the electorate is coerced by a minority of its members, that its position is like that of a man deliberately and entirely misled or confused. The matter is one of some complication, however, and we shall return to it.

It is also essential, essential to the freedom of electors to act on their politics, that there is no substantial limitation in law, or as a matter of entrenched principle, on what citizens can be candidates for office. The overwhelming majority can put themselves forward. In addition to this, again in order to secure the freedom of electors, there are no legal or conventionally established obstacles to campaigning. One must add that these possibilities of candidacy and campaigning are possibilities in more than law and general acceptance. They are to some extent generally available options, not privileges which can be exercised only by a minority, perhaps by the wealthy or by a group of men, united in ideology, who are the instruments of the wealthy.

Finally, again principally for the reason having to do with the freedom of electors to act on their politics, there is an effective prohibition on the coercion of candidates. The politics of candidates are not, in a certain sense, forced upon them.

To come now to *elections*, they are regular in democracies, and the electors make choices which are not coerced. The latter is partly secured through the institution of free voting: electors are able to register, can come to vote without apprehension, and, since we are not yet in John Stuart Mill's better world, can vote secretly. Their choices, one may add, are made in a tolerably rational fashion. They do not individuate candidates without reference to the politics of candidates, *merely* engaging in habitual responses of a kind suggested in certain 'realist' theories of political behaviour.

After an election the government is encouraged or restrained, but hardly controlled, not only by the evidence of the past election but also by the continuing articulation, by rising candidates and others, of popular attitudes and responses. These have an effect, partly, because they are indications of possible outcomes of the next election. Again there is the requirement that the electorate is not coerced. Its attitudes and responses are not forced upon it.

All of these features of the democratic practice, having to do with the politics of the electorate, candidacy and campaigning, with electoral choice, and with the exercise of influence after an election, make for what we may label as *the uncoerced choosing and influencing of government*. The label is attached to a group of criteria and is not to be construed as a description that might be applied to systems of government that do not in some degree satisfy the criteria. By the criteria as intended, our conception of democracy excludes the principal Communist states, whatever their virtues, and also certain conceivable states which as yet are a matter of hopeful or fearful speculation.

(ii) *Approximate equality*. To turn now to the second group of criteria, we must recall first that democracy gives to each of almost all adults the possibility of *one* vote in the choice of a government, and the possibility of some part, *not wholly out of line with the parts of others*, in the influencing of government. The second test is distressingly vague but we shall have to get along with it as stated. Here and elsewhere, this essay can be merely a précis. It is to be noticed that we do not require that each citizen can exercise *the same* influence, but only what might be called a tolerably similar one. Were we to do so, our conception would be remote from actual political systems, and inapposite for the discussion of them. The conception, as one can conclude from the fact of its appositeness, is also a relatively ordinary one, and hence has other advantages that typically go with ordinary conceptions.

In democracy, further, as might have been left implicit in what has been said, a system obtains whereby numbers of votes issue in an affinitive government: that is, an affinitive representative or number of representatives. The term 'affinitive representation' is preferable to what is more usual, 'proportionate representation'. It is a familiar fact that in our actual political systems a party may legitimately take power despite the fact that it has got less of the popular vote than an opposing party. There are other and more common facts of what can only be called *disproportion*. Things are different in the case of complete systems of Proportional Representation. In order to avoid a conception remote from actuality, let us speak of affinitive representation. Representation is affinitive, we may cursorily say, if it results from a procedure which gives to each vote an approximately equal weight.

We need not speak of a system of influence, a system for giving effect to popular attitudes between elections, that would be a counterpart of the system just mentioned for translating votes into representation. We can perhaps imagine possibilities in this area that would lead us to attempt to specify a safeguarding criterion.

We may bring together the criteria we have, pertaining mainly to 'one man, one vote', to the derivation of representation from votes, and to a similar influence on government of the wants and opinions of individuals between elections, under the label of *approximate equality of opportunity in the choosing and influencing of government*. The criteria have the consequence, which might once have affronted a cultural piety, that the Greek *polis* was not a democracy because of the exclusion of slaves and women from the franchise. There is also the obvious and satisfactory consequence that South Africa is a non-democratic state.

(iii) *Effective majority decision*. To come to criteria of the third group, the first of them requires that elected representatives take decisions of government as a result of majority vote. Hence there are many procedures of importance having to do with the business of elected assemblies and changes in government. It is of importance, secondly, that governmental decisions, like the politics and actions of candidates and electors, are not coerced. Minorities in the society do not force decisions upon government. To use a familiar analogy, and in anticipation of certain reflections about coercion to which we shall come, the government does not have a gun at its head.

It is to be noticed that satisfaction of the first condition obviously allows the possibility that there exists in society a 'permanent' minority. That is, there may be a group in society, united by race, religion or politics, whose representatives have no significant possibility of entering into coalition and hence majority. The condition may also be satisfied despite the existence of certain constitutional restraints on the majority. What are excluded by the requirement in question are certain powers of veto, effective control by non-elective upper houses, and so on.

Thirdly, we require of democracy that the decisions of representatives be translated into fact. A system may be a lesser approximation of democracy because of obstruction on the part of a bureaucracy or the courts. Again, a system may fail to be democratic, or fully democratic, because to some extent the rule of law does not prevail. The requirement of rule of law may be pitched so high that all the most likely political systems would, at certain times, fail to qualify as democracies. The requirement may also be pitched so low that something close to anarchy, in a true sense of that wildly abused word, would qualify. I intend to exclude both of these possibilities.

Our third group of criteria, about the procedures of elected assemblies and the efficacy of their decisions, may be labelled as criteria having to do with *effective majority decision by government*.

This, then, is an impression, if not much more than that, of the practice I shall have in mind in speaking of democracy. The conception in question, which will be clarified in some respects in the discussion that follows, is of use in discussing such systems of government as those in Britain and America. It is not, as I have said, utopian, a conception of an *ideal democracy*, but neither is it a conception that is fully satisfied in Britain or America or like societies. Certainly it does not describe the best conceivable practice of government. Some may consider that its full realization, or the full realization of a similar but higher conception of democracy, is the best we can hope for in actual political systems.

2 .Violence

Let us now spend some time, although not much, on the definition of violence and in particular of political violence. The question of definition, or what is too loosely called that, has been the subject of a bit of controversy, more than it is worth. In part, the controversy has been concerned with the kind of difficulties that beset any attempt to provide an analytical definition. That is, there have been the problems that arise in any attempt to capture, with respect to something, the definition of it which is implicit in ordinary usage and belief.[5] For example, should the definition of violence be so couched as to capture certain acts of speech?

In a second part, the controversy has had to do with attempts to press a definition wider than those that stand in some tolerable relation to ordinary usage and belief. We have been told that policemen, landlords, employers, shopkeepers, and indeed whole social classes and the state itself, engage in violence as a matter of course.[6] The fundamental suggestion, which has a considerable history, is not that policemen use more than the force allowed by their legal powers, that landlords send round thugs, or that the state engages in war and will use its army against revolution. Rather, it is that policemen, landlords and the state, in what most people regard as their peaceful conduct, are engaging in violence. This dispute is not essentially factual in character. It is not about established usage. We are given definitions issuing from political intention and required for simple *tu quoque* argument, whatever it may be worth. Such definitions enable the man who sets a bomb to reply to those who condemn him that they, too, engage in violence, perhaps the 'violence' which others of us might describe as unfairness, victimization or degradation.

In a third part, the so-called definitional controversy has to do with more idiosyncratic suggestions. It has been suggested, as we have seen,[7] that the 'distinctively political concept of violence' is to be eschewed because it is incoherent. It is so because of its connection with the notion of what a government or a state cannot morally have, a certain right to obedience. Again, the dispute is not essentially factual. The point stands, certainly, despite complications in the distinction between the factual and the evaluative.

Whatever sympathies one may have with the political intentions implicit in the second and third parts of the controversy, one may decline to take up the recommended usage or to be bound by the intended prohibition. If one sets out only to find a clear and unimpeding definition of violence, one which does not allow spurious victories to either Left or Right, there is relatively little difficulty.

An *act of violence*, we may briefly say, is a use of considerable or destroying force against people or things, a use of force that offends against a norm. This is not to presuppose, obviously, that in one's final verdict an act of violence must be wrong. There is not much to choose between this definition and several taken by philosophers from such good sources as the *Oxford English Dictionary*. There, an act of violence is one of physical force, inflicting injury or damage on persons or property. There is something to be said for our first definition, nonetheless. Its factual and evaluative parts are marked off, and it ranges across more acts than those of injury and damage. There would be, in other enterprises than our own, a need to give attention to the notion of a norm. Let us simply substitute 'law', in the sense of criminal law, for 'norm'. Also, we may add something else, since we are not concerned with merely criminal activity but with fire raisers, bomb setters, assailants and killers whose actions are of a political kind.

Let us then, as earlier in this book,[8] define *political violence* as *a considerable or destroying use of force against persons or things, a use of force prohibited by law and directed to a change in the policies, personnel or system of government, and hence to changes in society*. The definition covers such things as race riots, the destruction by fire and bomb of pubs and shops, kidnapping, hijacking, injuring, maiming and killing. It also encompasses revolutionary violence of the past. In specifying that the uses of force be directed to certain changes in policy or government, it does not require that the agents of violence have in view highly specific aims of change. Riots may count as political violence despite the absence of well-articulated intentions of the given kind and also despite their non-rational momentum.

3. Practice and rules

The first of the two questions raised at the beginning of this essay was that of how violence is related to the practice of democracy. That is, can one have a political system that can be said to satisfy the conception of democracy in some reasonable degree even though political violence occurs in the given society? The question depends for its sense, obviously, on the *level* of violence that is presupposed. The latter, in good part, is a matter of numbers of injuries and deaths, amount of damage and destruction. Let us have in mind only political violence at about the level of the violence in America and Europe over the past decade. Our question, although still large, is not a difficult one. It will nonetheless be advantageous in several ways, as I shall explain, to have a tolerably clear answer. In effect, what we shall come to have will be answers to a number of smaller questions. They will be more useful than any summation.

To find our smaller questions, let us look to the criteria of democracy, beginning with the first group, those pertaining to *the uncoerced choosing and influencing of government*. Violence need not stand in the way of candidacy and campaigning, regular elections and free voting. Violence, although it has brought appalling personal tragedy, does not in general impede or prevent these things. What of the requirements that electors and candidates are not coerced?

The requirements about coercion remain unclear and more will be said of them. However, it seems evident enough that they must be so defined that violence is excluded. In a situation where violence has forms of popular support, as it commonly does, it may certainly influence, direct or suborn electors. It must be regarded as conflicting with the criterion of democracy that electors are not coerced. It must also be granted that violence conflicts with the criterion pertaining to the non-coercion of candidates. We may conclude that violence at a certain level stands in the way of a system's greater satisfaction of the given criteria of democracy.

Consider now the requirements having to do with *approximate equality of opportunity in the choosing and influencing of government*. We may put aside, as not in conflict with violence, the requirement that numbers of votes produce affinitive representation. One of the other two requirements in this group is that each citizen has one vote. If we look at this with only an eye like the lens of a camera, it seems clear enough that violence is not in conflict with it. That is, violence is not generally a substantial impediment to each man's putting his ballot paper in the box or using the voting machine. To put this matter aside for a moment, there is the third criterion, to the effect that there is for each citizen a decently similar possibility of influencing the government, where that is principally a matter of giving evidence of political attitudes and inclinations. It seems true, or at any rate arguable, that political violence stands in the way of the adequate realization of this possibility. The possibility, looked at realistically, depends not only on such things as money for lobbying but also on the capability, preparedness and willingness of individuals to engage in certain lines of conduct. If a majority are in fact prevented, even if self-prevented, from engaging in acts of violence, then their possibility of influence is different from, and too much less than, that of a minority. Here, too, there is more to be said.

Let us look again at 'one man, one vote'. What is secured by this requirement? It is that each citizen has an equal rôle in that procedure, an election, which in a society without political violence has a certain large importance for governmental decisions. Equal rôles in the procedure recommend themselves because of the effectiveness of the procedure. The criterion of democracy that each citizen has one vote is important only because we assume something about the efficacy of the election. It is not unreasonable to conclude, perhaps, that a certain level of violence in a society, since it somewhat reduces the relative efficacy of voting, is in some conflict with the criterion of 'one man, one vote'. I do not mean to suggest that in recent experience the efficacy of elections has been much reduced.

Finally, there is the third group of criteria, having to do with *effective majority decision by government.* Political violence does not conflict with the first in this group, that representative assemblies take decisions by majority vote. As for the second, that governmental decisions are not coerced, political violence clearly does stand in the way of its fuller satisfaction. The last criterion of the group is that governmental decisions are effective, and hence that the rule of law prevails. Here, it is even more difficult to judge precisely. The principal difficulty is that of setting an upper limit on violence, beyond which violence is in substantial conflict with democracy. What can be said with assurance, but not very usefully, is that any system is less democratic in the given respect if there is such an incidence of violence as that with which we have become familiar in the past decade.

So much for one approach to our questions. Another must be made if we are to reach anything like a judicious view of how violence affects democracy. Other things also impede a fuller realization of the practice. We must be aware of them, and take them into account in a comparative view of the effect of violence. In this connection, it is clear enough that some uses of economic power ensure that systems of democracy only partially satisfy the criteria of democracy. Democracy has long been distinguished from plutocracy, in its several guises, and rightly so.

There can be no doubt that wealth, in itself and through its concomitants, makes for a coercion of electorate and candidates in their politics. The ways of this coercion are various and often covert. Constraining ideology, to mention only that, is not just a feature of alien systems. Secondly, it is clear enough that political uses of the power wielded by wealth prevent a fuller realization of the criteria having to do with equality of opportunity in the choosing and influencing of government. Dahl observed, of but one aspect of the American system, that 'if it could be quantified I suppose that Mr Henry Luce has a thousand or ten thousand times greater control over the alternatives scheduled for debate and tentative decision at a national election than I do'.[9] Mr Luce, of course, was a newspaper magnate. Thirdly, much the same situation exists in connection with the criteria of effective majority decision. The rule of law has in effect been broken through the systematic avoidance by businesses and individuals of the intended effects of legislation. In general, it is at least arguable that in every recent decade economic power has been *greatly* more effective than violence in keeping the British and American systems from being fuller realizations of democracy.

It nonetheless remains true, however balanced one's judgement, that violence does render such systems considerably less democratic than otherwise they might be. This involves the criteria concerned with ways of affecting the politics and actions of electorates and governments, with equality of opportunity in the choosing and influencing of governments, and with the rule of law.

My principal reason for clarifying this factual proposition, that violence does render systems less democratic, is to avoid a certain vagueness and confusion. We all believe that democracy and violence somehow conflict. It is important, however, to know exactly where they do conflict and where they do not, and not to confuse these places. We have one clear conflict before us. As I shall explain later, we must not make too much of this conclusion. It would be mistaken to make it decisive in the judgement of all political violence in democratic systems.

A lesser reason for clarifying the factual proposition about the practice of democracy and violence is to establish the weakness of unreflective and extravagant claims to the effect that acts of violence themselves *destroy* democracy. In general, they do not. They do less to make systems undemocratic than do acts of economic power.

It is also unreflective, incidentally, to succumb to the related generalization that political violence always poses a significant *threat* to the continuation of a democratic system of government. The supposition here is that violence, however it may conflict at some moment with this or that part of the system, always carries the significant threat of an unpredictable sequence of events ending in the destruction of the system. I shall have more to say that is relevant to this supposition. It represents, typically, an unconsidered attempt at restraint rather than a considered judgement. Indeed, the generalization that violence always threatens the existence of a democratic system is at about the level of clarity and credibility of the generalization that a democratic system always threatens its own existence. Collapses of democratic systems have as often been brought about by their own passivities as by political violence.

Let us now turn to the question raised at the beginning of this essay about the rules of democracy. How does political violence stand in relation to them? We can deal with the matter quickly, partly for the reason that we already have the rules of democracy before us. They have emerged in the description of the democratic practice, since the most economical way of describing it is principally by way of its rules. Also, the question of violence and the rules of democracy is in a way more tractable than that of violence and the ongoing reality of democracy. Many of the rules of democracy, as we have conceived it, are not determinate. Still, it is easier to conclude that behaviour counts as an infraction of a rule than to decide, as a result of certain behaviour, how far one must qualify a general description of a system which is a complex structure of rules and indeed more than that.

Guided by our findings about political violence and systems, we can conclude about political violence that it breaks the rule of democracy that electors and candidates are not to be coerced, and also the rule that each citizen is to have one vote, where that is understood to require equal participation in a fundamental procedure which gives rise to political decisions. Violence may be said to break the latter rule because the relative efficacy of the procedure is reduced. Thirdly, violence may be said to break the rule of democracy that each citizen is to have an approximately equal rôle in the influencing of governments, where what is in question is something other than voting. Fourthly, violence breaks the rule of democracy that governmental decisions are to be taken as binding, that the rule of law is to prevail.

We thus have a second clear conflict between violence and democracy. Violence breaks rules of the practice. This is unaffected by another fact, whatever else may be thought of it, and however it may enter into different arguments, that non-violent infractions of the rules of democracy have been more substantial than violent infractions. Non-violent infractions deriving from wealth and from class ascendancies have been greatly more numerous and effective than violent infractions. It is worth remarking, too, that acts of violence break rules of which there is in fact some observance. It is not as if they 'broke' rules that have been *destroyed* by infractions deriving from economic power, or rules that can be said to have always been circumvented by oppressing classes, as the Left sometimes supposes.

As in the case of the first conflict, our conclusion here must not be taken for too much. It is clear that there is no direct and unquestionable passage from the premise of something's being against a rule to the conclusion that it is wrong. That is a part of what we must now consider.

4. Arguments and ends

The rules of democracy are no more than rules, and they do not give one what they imperfectly imply, the arguments for democracy. If one wants to know what is to be said for democracy, and how that is related to other things, one must look elsewhere than the rules. In part they are no more than means for securing ends which are cited in the arguments. The situation is familiar. If one wants to know what is to be said for keeping one's promise, one does not find it, except inchoately, in the rules of promising. The overall rule that one must do as one promises does not give a justification for doing as one promises. That has to do with the effects of the rule.

The arguments for democracy are sometimes collected into a disorder. Here we are offered the traditional liberties or the rule of law or the virtues of the democratic personality, there the efficiency of free-enterprise economies, here governmental stability and there the progress of science. Better can be done, I think, and without the distortion that sometimes results from a kind of reductionism. There appear to be two fundamental grounds for the practice and rules of democracy. They both have to do in several ways with the Principle of Equality and hence the ideal of well-being for all.

Arguments from both these grounds have to do with the democratic practice itself and also with consequences of the practice, whether or not they are also consequences of other practices. It is no doubt a mistake to attempt to *define* the democratic practice by means of rights, policies, customs and benefits that generally go with it but are logically distinct from it. But, although such things are connected with the practice only contingently, they do enter into its justification. If democracies invariably, or even very often, went along with continual economic failure or a denial of non-political rights, we would have very much less to say for democracies.

One principal argument for democracy is that, compared to other practices, it gives less autonomy to any individual or minority in determining the policies of a society. Most importantly, it gives less to that minority which is made up of the governing representatives. To accept this, we need not depend on such supports as Plato's taxonomy of political systems, but on the evident nature of contemporary alternatives to democracy. We may, as a consequence of reasonable argument concerning such things as 'intra-party democracy' in the Soviet Union, be made to hesitate. We may be made to hesitate, too, by those many accusations, including the Marxist one, concerning privileged classes and minorities in our democracies. Indeed, we must amend a great deal of received doctrine. But it remains clear enough that the practice of democracy gives less autonomy to any individual or minority than do alternative forms of government.

It is to be noticed that democracy is *not* being recommended as denying the mentioned autonomy to an individual or a minority *and* giving it to ordinary people who make up the society. Such a claim is patently at odds with the facts. The people do not *rule*, and they never have. Democracy gives to citizens only something which can best be described briefly in a negative way: a circumstance in which no individual or minority has as much autonomy, with respect to major policies of the society, as have individuals or minorities in other political practices. It gives to citizens not any freedom *of* power but rather a freedom *from* power. The practice does this as a consequence of certain of its features enumerated at the beginning of this essay. I shall not attempt to relate this general contention, about the general absence of an autonomy in major policies, to many related praisings of democracy, some of which are wonderfully inflated.

We have so far considered only a possible autonomy which is a power to determine the policies of a society. In a democracy, no individual or minority has it. There are, however, other possible autonomies which in fact are realized in a democracy, or realized to some extent. These are smaller and yet enter importantly into the present fundamental argument for democracy. The argument has to do with the satisfaction and the distress of individuals, in considerable part the satisfaction of freedom and the distress of a want of freedom.

Some of these autonomies are integral to the practice, as defined, and are secured by what are known as the political rights. How a man will vote *is* within his decision, and his satisfaction in its being so is real. Others of these smaller autonomies are consequences rather than integral parts of the democratic practice, although not invariably so, and are in part secured by non-political rights. Here we have freedoms of culture, including religion, and freedom in the use of law. Also among the consequences of democracy are certain individual possibilities for the possession and use of natural and produced goods, both material and otherwise. This recommendation, having to do with a kind of production, is not one that is peculiar to democracy, as some of our economists have so long suggested. It seems a probability that the Soviet Union will come to have something very like it, and as probable that its not having had it in the past cannot be quickly explained by the non-democratic nature of its political system. Still, the existence of these possibilities for the possession and use of goods *is* a fact about democratic societies and hence a recommendation of them.

One fundamental argument for democracy, then, is that it secures to citizens a freedom from a certain possible power, and also secures or allows to them an array of lesser freedoms. They exercise small powers and realize certain possibilities of possession and use. This we may call *the argument of freedom*. It is related to the other fundamental ground of support for democracy, but the two are logically distinct in important ways.

One can advance the argument of freedom, correctly, on behalf of a society disfigured by extreme differences or disparities in individual powers and possibilities. Necessarily, if the argument can be used reasonably, the society is not any form of tyranny. That is, its major policies are not within the decision of an individual ruler or a minority of rulers. Nonetheless, there is no difficulty about supposing that the society in question, while it can be said to accord the lesser possibilities and powers to all, in fact distributes them in a grossly unequal way. Obviously enough, a man may truly be said to have freedoms without its being true, by some comparative test, that he has enough of them. There are situations where for two men to have a certain freedom, it must be that each has as much as the other. This is not generally so, and it is not so in the case of freedoms of the kind we are considering.

The second argument for democracy, as may be anticipated, is *the argument of equalities*. It is that in a democracy one gets certain approximations to equality. Some of them are greater approximations than in non-democratic societies, others are lesser approximations. These approaches to equality, full realizations of equality in several instances, are to be found in the democratic practice itself and also in its customary consequences.

With respect to the practice, it *is* a necessary truth that if no individual or minority has autonomy with respect to the society's policies, then all have equal freedom from such autonomy. In this case, evidently, there does exist a logical connection between a freedom and its equal distribution. Even here, for good reason, we may distinguish between freedom and an equal sharing in it.

In the case of lesser freedoms which are also integral to the democratic practice, there is a closer approximation to equality than in the case of whatever analogous freedoms exist in alternative practices. In this case, the equalities in question are not entailed by the very existence of the freedoms. About this and other comparisons with alternative practices of government, incidentally, it is worth remarking that there is good reason to concentrate on those practices that have been realized and whose nature is known. There is good reason for the common reluctance to give as much attention to those alternatives which as yet are no more than objects of speculation.

The argument of equalities, as noted, also concerns the freedoms which are not integral to the practice of democracy. Some of them are more equally distributed in non-democratic than in democratic societies. I have in mind approximations to economic and social equality, and all that goes with those approximations. This is a large fact, and indeed it provides an argument against democratic societies which cannot be much diminished. It is nevertheless not an argument which carries the day. No single argument can. In the case of certain other freedoms not integral to democracy, freedoms of culture and law, democracy does better than its alternatives.

These, then, are the two fundamental arguments for the practice of democracy. We shall have to leave unconsidered what appears to be the virtue of taking freedom and equalities as grounds of democracy rather than beginning from principles of justice.[10] We shall also leave untouched, as I have already implied, the relationship of the two arguments to a number of derivative defences of democracy.[11]

The remaining question raised at the beginning of this essay was that of how political violence stands to the arguments for democracy. More particularly, how does it stand to the *ends* presupposed in these arguments? These are political and related freedoms, and equalities in these things. While democratic systems do usually make for some realization of the specified ends, they do not always do so. Historically speaking, democratic systems have not always advanced progress towards these elements of well-being. They have sometimes impeded that progress. This has had to do, in part, with permanent minorities, non-accredited groups in pluralist systems, and the failure of democratic governments to respond to the intensity of distress, as distinct from its extent. It is an obvious fact that democracy has not always served progress towards the ends of Blacks in America and Catholics in the province of Ulster. This has been a question of some of the forms of freedom and some of the forms of equality. Also, of course, considerable impediments to progress have been raised up by undemocratic means.

I do not mean to suggest, however, that democratic systems have failed only in certain very isolated instances to serve these two large objectives. If one turns one's attention away from political and civil rights and the like, and thinks of the distribution of material goods and the consequences of that distribution, one encounters larger facts, general facts of inequality and suffering. The whole of the record of democratic systems is dark.

There inevitably is the proposition, then, that precisely the ends of the arguments for the practice of democracy can also be used to support departures from it. The ends which are thought to be served by the rules of democracy are at least sometimes served by the breaking of the rules. This is as plain as the fact that one sometimes serves the ultimate ends of making a promise by *not* doing what one has promised to do. There is a further point. It can be argued that in some cases the *only* infractions which do effectively serve the ends of democracy are acts of political violence. The argument is in part that nothing else will work, or that nothing else will work in a reasonable time. A morally insupportable distance between privilege and deprivation will not be appreciably reduced in one lifetime, or two, by a commitment to only certain ways of affecting electorates, to 'one man, one vote', to an approximate equality in the influencing of government, and to the rule of law.

Will anyone persist in thinking that if the argument of freedom and the argument of equalities do give support to democracy, it cannot be that the ends presupposed by those arguments can enter into an argument for violent infraction of the rules of democracy? There is no reason for thinking so, no inconsistency. If one considers other practices, small and large, it is evident enough that sometimes their justifying purposes are served by departing from them. Kindness in personal relations is usually but certainly not always done by sticking to certain rules of conduct. It is familiarity that certain rules do generally serve ends of fairness but that occasions arise when precisely the ends of fairness are to be achieved only by making an exception to the rules.

I leave out, in all of this, and it is a lot left out, the claims of individuals who are not members of the societies on which we are fixing attention, our own societies, but of other societies. If the ends of the fundamental arguments for democracy can enter into a consideration of violence which has to do with the deprivation of members of our own societies, these ends can also enter into a consideration of violence which has to do with aggression against individuals in other societies.

5. Democratic violence

It could not be the intention of any sane person to suggest a general justification of political violence. It would be as irrational to do so as to offer a general justification of all uses of force by the state, against its own subjects or others. I do not contemplate, either, any general acceptance of political violence of the Left. What seems to me true, although beyond being shown here, is that there is a justification of some political violence. There is, most relevantly, a moral justification for *some* of what I shall call *democratic violence*. Any violence so named is to be understood as having certain characteristics, and these will play a considerable part in any justification it may have.

One of these features has just been given. It can be said for some political violence that it serves large ends of freedom and equality. One may argue for, although not necessarily justify, such violence as serving the ends which are also the ends of the practice of democracy, a practice which by definition is non-violent. Thus the fundamental arguments for the practice of democracy may also be used in defence of some political violence. Other types of violence, including almost all violence of the Right, cannot call upon these arguments. The proposition that violence does as a matter of fact promote progress towards freedom and equality in some circumstances can hardly be questioned. The nostrum that nothing is gained by violence does not survive a moment's reflection. It is remarkable, despite its service to entrenched interests, and to the *amour propre* of democratic politicians, that it persists at all.

The fact about ends is a considerable one, partly because the ends in question are not external to the democratic practice but internal to it. They inform the practice and are fundamental to its character. Furthermore, although the question is a large one, it may be argued that it is *uniquely* the democratic practice that is effectively directed towards both these ends. It is not as if some violence were directed towards ends of democracy, but ends not of its nature, or directed to ends of democracy clearly shared with other practices of government.

Nonetheless, we have in the fact about ends only one characteristic of democratic violence, one of five. We have, as well, only a necessary condition of the reasonableness of naming some violence as democratic. The argument does not depend on nomenclature, but if no more could be said, there would be justice in the reply that once again a term of honour was being misappropriated. More can be said.

A part of it has to do with a notion which has so far been used in this essay but hardly examined. We have seen that the democratic practice, in several ways, excludes *coercion*. A part of what is excluded, as we have granted, is violence. Let us put this aside for a moment and consider a general and fundamental separation of kinds of coercion. These may be called the coercion of force and the coercion of persuasion.

The *coercion of force* is exemplified by (i) my remaining in a room because I am bound and gagged, (ii) my giving up my wallet in the street at the point of a gun, and (iii) my injuring a man rather than allowing a number of men to be tortured or to die. In the first case talk of my *acting*, and my *doing* anything, is out of place, but the case is relevant to our concerns nonetheless. It is true in an important way, in all three cases, although for different reasons, that I am not left room for effectual reflection and judgement about what I do. This is so in the first case because only one thing, not even an action, is physically possible. It is true in the second case because only one action is possible, given a limit on human capability which we all accept. I could try to keep my wallet, but only at a risk which I am not expected to take. I am left no room for effectual judgement in the third case either. Only one action is possible, at least if the situation is not complicated in certain ways, given a moral prohibition which has quite general acceptance.

It is evident enough that these three cases differ in a certain respect. The first involves a single physical possibility, the second a single human possibility, and the third a single moral possibility. They are alike in that they offer but a *single* possibility and hence that there is no room for effectual reflection and judgement. As a consequence of this, although the fact is of secondary importance to us, I am absolved from a certain responsibility in each case. I may be responsible for an act which gave rise to any of the situations, but that is irrelevant. The third case raises various questions, but it is surely true, in an important sense, that I would not be held responsible for injuring the man.

The *coercion of persuasion* can be illustrated by my giving an unwilling donation to a dubious charity when I believe that the collector will mention a refusal to my employer, who is in favour of the charity. Another example of the coercion of persuasion is my not intervening in a man's denigrating talk about my friend since I believe the man has just been upset by a personal affront. I am restrained, not willingly, by my belief about his state of mind. My restraint may or may not appear to me to have a moral ground. In both cases, I am left room for effectual reflection and judgement.

I do not wish to assert that there is a distinction of a certain kind between the coercion of force and the coercion of persuasion. That is, I do not wish to assert that there is a criterion such that all instances of coercion fall clearly into one category or the other. It would be surprising if this were true. Many instances *do* fall into one category or the other, and this is sufficient for my argument. I do not suppose either, of course, that the two coercions have been fully analysed or all questions about them answered.

To return to the relevant criteria of democracy, it is evident that they require that the electorate as a whole not be subject to the coercion of force. If an electorate is subject to the coercion of force, the system of government in question is necessarily a tyranny. It is, indeed, principally because of the obvious need to distinguish democracy from tyranny that the criteria of democracy pertaining to coercion appear to be, as they are, unquestionable.

However, are the criteria to be understood in such a way that the electorate in a democracy cannot be subject to the coercion of persuasion, in any form? If they are so understood, then no existing system of government is within sight of satisfying the criteria and none ever has been. The practice of democracy is such that it is possible for minorities and interest groups to exert pressure on the electorate. These pressures sometimes stand in analogy with those persuasions of individuals mentioned above. They sometimes evoke moral responses and sometimes evoke responses of prudence, but not what we may call enforced prudence. It is hardly too much to say that the democratic practice has at its bottom the coercion of persuasion. The electorate is restrained or constrained, but in such a way that it is left room for reflection. The same is true for candidates and governments.

It may be supposed, at this point, that violence conflicts with democracy, as we have seen it does, because it consists, always, in the coercion of force. It does not. Some violence consists in the coercion of persuasion.

Governments, to speak first of them, are left room for effectual reflection and decision in the face of this violence. The American government was not *forced*, by acts of violence, to enter into a more vigorous policy against racial discrimination and racism. It was certainly not *forced* by violence, although the point takes us out of the area of our primary concern, to change its policy of war in Vietnam. The British government was not *forced* to take seriously the demands of the oppressed minority in Ulster. A man whose shop is destroyed by a fire or a bomb, or a man who abandons his shop in the face of the direct threat of fire or bomb, *is* subjected to the coercion of force. Such facts, and also the facts of injury and death, must enter into reflection and count against violence. It remains true that governments are not subjected to the coercion of force by such acts. The case is similar with electorates and with candidates. With few exceptions, they are not forced into their politics by violence or forced into particular political behaviour.

We have it, then, that while violence is excluded by the criteria of democracy having to do with coercion, it cannot be that these criteria exclude the coercion of persuasion. It follows, then, that violence is not excluded as being coercion of persuasion. The exact ground is different, and not now important to us.

To come to the principal point, some violence shares an attribute with procedures allowed by the criteria of democracy, procedures which are basic to democratic systems. Some violence is a matter of the coercion of persuasion. It is fundamentally different from behaviour which leaves no option to electorates, candidates and governments. The second feature of democratic violence, then, is just this, that it consists only in the coercion of persuasion and so shares an attribute with activity that is integral to the democratic practice.[12]

The third characteristic of democratic violence has to do with equalities. It has been granted that political violence conflicts with the criteria of democratic practice which require an approximation to equality of influence for all citizens. Violence may give to individuals who engage in it a greater degree of influence than is enjoyed by some of the majority of individuals who do not engage in it. It was granted, too, that violence breaks other equality-rules of the democratic practice. Still, there is another consideration. Of the individuals who do not engage in violence, as we have noticed, there are some who enjoy very great inequalities of influence. That is, wealth and position give to some considerable number of individuals a far greater influence than is had by almost all of those individuals who are without wealth or position. Let us compare, then, the group of the violent and the group of the privileged. It is plain enough that the violent may be seen as attempting to secure an equal influence or something like it. For the most part, they do not succeed.

It must be admitted that the violent are securing or attempting to secure a favourable inequality when compared with a majority of the citizens of their society. This proposition is a ground for our conclusions concerning criteria and rules. It will be of some importance, too, in any final assessment of violence. At the same time, it is entirely relevant that violence by another comparison may be an attempt to secure *equality* of influence, or an approximation of it. All of this, needless to say, is of a schematic character and could do with improvement of several kinds. The result of a more extended examination, I suggest, will be a conclusion of the kind we have. It is that some violence has an affinity with a feature of the democratic practice. A criterion of that practice is that there is an approximation to equality of influence. Some violence, by one important comparison, is an attempt to approximate more closely to an equality of influence.

A fourth characteristic of democratic violence is that it is *not* directed to the destruction of a democratic system. This is true of most of the violence with which we are familiar. It is not revolutionary in reality, whatever the accompanying rhetoric. That is, it does not have as its object the establishment of a radically different system, one that is non-democratic. In this respect, it is similar to almost all civil disobedience. To suppose that all violence is revolutionary, and that all violence in democratic systems is aimed at the overthrow of those systems, is to fly in the face of the evidence of the present and the past.

There is also a fifth characteristic, related to the fourth. It is not merely that violence of the kind I have in mind is not directed to the destruction of democratic systems, but that its effects are likely to be that the systems in question become fuller realizations of democracy in certain respects. That this has been the consequence of violence in the historical development of a number of governmental systems is as established a fact as that democratic systems have had their beginnings in revolutionary violence.

Violence, then, may serve the ends which are fundamental to the democratic practice. Secondly, it may, as coercion, share an attribute with procedures that are intrinsic to democratic systems. It cannot be said without dismay and apprehension, but it is to be said that some bombs are like votes. Thirdly, this violence is by one comparison an attempt to gain equality of influence. Fourthly, it is not directed to the ending of democratic systems. It may, finally, lead to their becoming more democratic.

6. Justification

To review the entire course of this essay, we began with the practice of democracy and with political violence, and passed on to a number of propositions. (i) Political violence renders the system of government of a society less democratic, as to a greater extent do certain uses of economic power. This is one conflict between democracy and violence. (ii) Political violence conflicts with certain of the rules of democracy. Although the same is true of economic power, we here have a second conflict between democracy and violence. (iii) Some violence, as we have just seen, may serve the very ends of the fundamental arguments for the practice of democracy. Here, it is mistaken to find conflict. Some of the violence in question, further, has other features of as much importance. It may be named democratic violence.

This latter part of this exercise in particular has relevance to the general question of the justification of political violence. That is, I have not pointed to similarity between the democratic practice and one kind of political violence of the Left, democratic violence, only in order to establish the fact of similarity. Rather, it has been my intention to bring into clearer view something that will make less difficult our judgement of political violence. It seems true that in considering problematic behaviour, it is a great advantage if we can see clearly its relations to unproblematic behaviour. If in personal relations a man acts in an ambiguous way, and his action requires some kind of appraisal, that appraisal will be facilitated by our seeing to what extent his action has the character of a threat, say, or a warning. It is when his action cannot be assimilated to anything which already has been the subject of reflection and judgement that there is the greatest difficulty.

Some political violence has features that are shared with the practice of democracy, and that practice, for all that can be said against it, has a large recommendation. These are facts of which we are morally obliged to take account. We have in them one reasoned connection between facts about our societies, the facts of inequality, and substantial conclusions about political violence.

I have said that it seems to me that at least some violence has a moral justification, but I have not *shown* this. It will be clear, I trust, that I do not suppose that the proposition that some violence has a justification can be derived from the fact alone that it is in the given sense democratic. To think violence can be justified this way is as mistaken as taking as a justification of a policy the fact by itself that the policy issues from the democratic practice. If some bombs are like votes, they also maim and kill. The deprivation and degradation that call up violence must not be absent from thought and feeling, and not so present in them as to obscure other terrible realities.

5 FOUR CONCLUSIONS ABOUT POLITICAL VIOLENCE OF THE LEFT

It is a terrible fact of this time, not much lessened by there having been similar facts in the past, or by the likelihood of there being more in the future, that men make use of destructive force against persons and things, force condemned by ordinary law but directed to changing societies in certain ways. Certain of these changes in societies, although typically they are sought for themselves, may be taken to make for progress towards a certain goal, well-being for all persons without exception, all persons in whatever societies. The uses of force related in this way to the goal of a general well-being are of course political violence of the Left. My purpose in this last essay is to say some things in advocacy of a certain response, in good part a sceptical one, to the general moral question of what is to be said against such violence, and what for it.

1. Political obligation

Political obligation, of which we know something already,[1] belies its traditional name, since it is the moral obligation to act legally, our moral obligation to act in accordance with ordinary law. More precisely, members of a society are morally obliged to act in certain ways for a reason involving the fact that these are the legal ways. Members of a society ought to act so as to obey the laws of the society for a reason having to do in some way or other with the existence of the laws. They are not to act in other ways for a reason having to do with their illegality. This is distinct from any reason for not acting in those ways which does not have to do with the law, such as the plain reasons that to act in those ways may in itself and directly cause pointless suffering or be vicious or unjust, this having nothing to do with illegality. It is important that political obligation, so-called, be distinguished from other moral obligations bearing on the same legal or illegal conduct, obligations which would exist in the absence of ordinary law, and hence if the conduct were neither legal nor illegal.

Some seem to think, still, that the general moral question of political violence can be settled by citing the fact of political obligation. Let us consider something more of this, in the main because it is a means to something else. Certainly there are large propositions about political obligation in the history of political philosophy, they have been paid much attention, and they are still relied on. There is not much, indeed, that is more relied on.

Hobbes may be taken to say that we ought to keep the law, and certainly not contemplate the setting of bombs for political ends, because of the terribleness of the alternative, which he calls a state of war. A decent existence depends on forswearing an individualism, on accepting the restraints of legality. Breaking the law carries the danger of leading to a state of war. He may be taken to say, further, that as a result of the threat of this alternative, members of a society must consent among themselves to give an absolute monopoly of force to the state, and in fact all of us have entered into such a covenant, or anyway find ourselves in one willy-nilly. That is, we are in a covenant to obey the law, the state's law. The state's enjoyment of its monopoly is not conditional on its ruling in accordance with any agreed terms. It is not a party to the covenant, which is among us members of the society.[2]

From Locke there is the different proposition that the members of certain societies, those which are not subject to tyranny, ought to keep the laws of the societies, and certainly not resort to violence, since the alternative, if not necessarily so bad as Hobbes's state of war, is a lesser good, some hurt to the general interest, some reduction in the goods of civil society. In fact we members of such societies do give our tacit consent to forswear violence and all illegality. The state, for its part, must respect and protect our natural rights.[3] In Rousseau, perhaps, there are similar arguments. However, like others of his thoughts, they are obscured in his grand vision of society, its past, present and future.[4]

What we have, in Hobbes and Locke at least, are two arguments for the existence of an obligation to obey the law. One is of a Utilitarian sort, that illegality will bring in its train some catastrophe or some loss of goods. To break the law is to endanger a beneficial order. The other argument is that we have made a contract or covenant to obey the law, or that we have given our consent. Let us first look at this second sort of argument. In considering it, of course, we shall not contemplate any merely imaginable or hypothetical contract, any contract other than an actual one. Rawls's method of argument for two principles of justice and for political obligation, as we know,[5] includes an imaginable contract. Imaginable contracts, whatever use they may be in inquiry into moral and political principles, and into non-contractual obligation, clearly give rise to no *contractual* obligations whatever on our part. That is, they do not give rise to anything like an obligation deriving from the making of an agreement.

Let us examine the possibility of there being a contract between individuals and their state or society. What any contract comes to, at bottom, is that offers were made and were accepted by the two parties to the agreement. (i) How does an individual offer, to the society in which he lives and to the state under which he lives, to obey the law? (ii) How do the society and state accept his offer? (iii) How do they offer, and (iv) how does he accept, whatever it is that they offer to him, presumably the common goods of civil society?

The principal question of these four is the first one, about an individual's offer to his society and state. An answer derived from Locke comes to this: that an individual's tacit offer consisted in the accepting of social goods. Whatever else may be said of this, one clear thing is that *the act of accepting something*, in and by itself, is not an offer of any kind, tacit or otherwise. Nothing will turn an act of accepting, by itself, into the making of an offer. (Any doubt about this can be put to rest by imagining acts of accepting something, say a gift or a payment, in various other contexts.) Can we get any further ahead by considering not acts of accepting, but acts of participating in government, or related acts, say *voting in a democratic election*? Let us think of just the latter, voting, which has sometimes been taken as akin to offering.[6] Voting, evidently, is expressing a preference for one of a small number of general policies for a society, or, better, one of a number of would-be governments. One thing to be said of it, as of accepting something, is that in and by itself it is not offering. To express a preference is not in and by itself to make an offer. This simple truth, like the other one, has too often gone unstated and perhaps unnoticed.

Certainly it is possible, in special contexts, for an accepting of goods or the casting of a vote (or just moving one's fingers, or a bit of dancing, or doing a job, or just standing still) to *count as* something else as well, such as an offer. This depends, as we all know, on there being a certain prior understanding. More particularly, the fact of an offer or whatever depends on a prior act or activity by the agent, perhaps an utterance, precisely to the effect that this subsequent voting or whatever is also to count as something else. It is possible for there to be a dispute as to whether there did in fact occur the essential prior act or activity. It is just possible for there to be argument, I suppose, to the conclusion that each of us has acted in such a way as to convey that our acceptings of social goods, or our votings, are to count as offers to obey the law. Any such argument or speculation will surely be weak stuff.

I shall not consider any, but simply make a proposal which may produce conviction. It seems to have the virtue of conceding what needs to be conceded, if anything at all is to be saved of the sorry history of suppositions and doctrines about an actual social contract. Also, it goes a good way towards explaining that history. (If *no* explanation could be offered of the thing, one would of course have a reason for suspecting that one had missed a good argument, or anyway *an* argument.) The proposal has to do with *a general expectation* rather than an agreement, and hence it has to do with something that has often been confused with an agreement. This is so since agreements, among other things, do certainly create expectations. This general expectation has something to do with the existence of plain and clear offers of various kinds, so far unmentioned, and also with accepting benefits and voting, and with something else more important than any of these.

Members of societies make many offers that certainly are *related* to the offer on their part which is required by the Contract Argument, as we may call it, for political obligation. Many prospective employees offer, in addition to their work, a certain general conduct, more or less in line with legality. In modern societies, further, a good many of the many people in question are prospective employees of the state. The offer is an unquestionable and ordinary one, part of a legal contract. So with the offers of individuals who enter into contracts having to do with the hiring of property. There are also related offers made in connection with memberships of various kinds, and with such episodes as travel. What we have in these things is a large fact. It is that we make many offers of good behaviour or better. They are not often the offer of total legality for the indefinite future, which is what is supposed in the Contract Argument, but they carry us some way in that direction.

My suggestion is that this ramified fact of our many ordinary offers, and to a lesser extent our acceptings of social goods, and to a still lesser extent our votings, contribute to *a general expectation*: the expectation on the part of our fellows that we will obey the law. The expectation, which derives above all from yet another thing, which is the plain fact of our customary behaviour, is at its strongest in connection with the law against violence. Given this general expectation, breaking the law gives rise to frustration, outrage and shock. No one will think, I trust, that to create an expectation that one will do a thing *is* always somehow to agree to do it. One *can* create an expectation without its being true that doing it depends on an accepted conventional procedure to be gone through by two parties correctly and completely.[7] Only if the latter is true, as it is when one makes an offer, or does something that counts as one, and so on, does the expectation derive from a contract.

In this general expectation and its possible frustration, we have something clear in support of the idea that we have an obligation to obey the law. This, I suggest, is pretty well the residue of the prolonged speculation about a social contract. This is what we can keep. The best description of our situation is not in part that we have made what counts as an offer, on which some of us may go back, but that we have contributed to a general expectation, which some of us may defeat. It remains the best description when we add in useful considerations having to do with the acceptances of our many lesser offers, by such parties as employers, and the supposed offer from the other side, by the state or society, and our supposed acceptance of it.[8]

The residue we have is not nothing, but perhaps it comes to very little. It may be a small thing when compared with others, some of which are also arguments against violence, and some of which are arguments in favour of violence. To come to the point quickly, and by way of an analogy, there is the simple truism that the prospective frustration of a class of slave-owners, when their general expectation that the slaves will not rise is defeated, places no noticeable obligation on the slaves not to rise. It is a general truth that what the frustration of any expectation counts for is a matter of what else is on hand. There *may* be much larger things on hand, misery or great distress or exploitation or injustice. Obligations having to do with these larger things will then defeat the obligation not to give frustration, or overwhelm it. On the other hand, there may be obligations which do not conflict with, but which need no support from, the given obligation having to do with the defeat of expectation. They are, so to speak, greater forces in the same direction, against violence. They too may have to do with misery, distress, exploitation or injustice.

Let us leave the Contract Argument for a time and consider more quickly the other reason for political obligation derived from Hobbes and Locke. It is, in one form, that the illegality of an act, as distinct from any other feature, increases the probability of a catastrophe or the loss of certain goods. This Utilitarian reason, of course, can be advanced independently of the Contract Argument.[9] Taken just as it is, this reason for political obligation does pretty well require that we make judgements about such larger things as those just mentioned, misery and the like. The Contract Argument for political obligation may be taken to promise *an effective argument* against violence, to promise that we can avoid certain questions about these larger things, but in fact, as we have seen, it may be that we cannot. This is clearer, certainly, when it is seen that what is in question is not really a contract or agreement but only an expectation. The second line of reasoning does not offer such a promise. Speculation about an act's illegality leading to a catastrophe or a loss of goods inevitably brings in the opposed speculation about the act's possible gains. There is its possible contribution, *still taken as an illegality*, to ending or alleviating misery and the like. That is also possible. There is also another clear point, related to what was said of the residue of the Contract Argument. Whatever speculations we come to about illegality and its dangers and gains, they may be at least well-matched in importance by others. In a sentence, there may be at least as much to be said *against* my act taken simply as a killing, in itself and for its direct consequences, as when it is taken as something which may have certain consequences as an illegality. In another sentence, it may be that there is something to be said *for* an act of mine, considered in connection with large things, gains of justice or humanity, and that this is of greater importance than what can be said against it as something which as an illegality may have certain consequences.

There remain some other possible reasons for political obligation, reasons which may deserve more attention than they have got. They are that there is fairness or repayment of debt or simply equality in obeying the law if one has accepted social goods or if one has participated to some extent in a certain decision-procedure, perhaps voted in a democratic election.[10] Here too, however, there may be no possibility of having an effective argument, of avoiding large questions. If so, this will again be a matter of who has what amounts of social goods, and who has what amounts of their opposites, or a matter of the extent to which elections have in fact been fair to all voters or members of society. One wonders if the Contract Argument has been so much to the forefront, as against these other possible reasons for political obligation, because it seemed not to raise the large questions.

2. Moral necessities

Consider people of a reflective and enlightened kind, people moved by the great ideal of the Left, well-being for all. Now consider proposing to them that in the aid of progress towards social changes taken to be in accord with the ideal of the Left, they shoot men down, or set bombs to kill and maim, or that they give money to an organization which does this. Consider advancing to them an argument of this predictable form: that the probable and the certain consequences of inaction or of non-violent action are such that violence, with all of its probable and certain consequences, is justified. Some of the people in question would reply along certain lines, in a certain manner and style, rather as follows.

It is wholly wrong to engage in attempting to weigh up what cannot be weighed up. Killing a man, killing a woman, maiming a child, destroying a family, these are atrocities which cannot be brought into a calculation of gains and losses. The things themselves are by nature inhuman or savage. It cannot be that there are common units in terms of which they are to be assigned a value. This cannot be done in terms of one category, the satisfaction of desires, as Utilitarians have thought, or in terms of some few states of feeling or of mind. These things cannot be reduced to subtraction and addition of human experience, efficiently categorized and balanced against uncertain futures. They are outrages, and outrages are not to be measured against anything.

Precisely the large-scale horrors of recent decades have resulted from attempts to do this. It is this computational morality which issued in the grisliness of the war against Vietnam and in earlier purges and massacres, and, in so far as it matters, in the bestialization of those who carried them out. One must have an overwhelming pessimism about the attempt to reason in this calculative way.

There is in fact no alternative to a morality of *necessities*: of what must be done, and what must not be done. This is not merely a matter of what *ought* to be done, and what *ought not* to be done, since moral necessities are more than merely imperatives. They have to do with the taking of life, sexual relations and relations of loyalty, the administration of justice, customs of respect and gentleness, and other things. Together they constitute the foundation of a human way of life, something needed in order to be human. We may have differences of judgement about them, but not to grant the existence of such necessities is to be other than human.

If these necessities can come into conflict in abnormal, painful and improbable situations, they are absolute nonetheless, and they can be so without benefit of religion or superstition. They have a truth, the truth of the human and the profoundly natural.

Chief among the necessities are those having to do with not taking life, respect for individual life, a horror of killing. The proposal, then, to kill the undefended or to support this killing, for purposes of generalized well-being, is unthinkable. To do so would be to be degraded in a way not to be affected at all by political success.

This response to political violence has been in a way derived from Stuart Hampshire's lecture, 'Morality and Pessimism',[11] although the lecture is of wide scope and does not mention political violence. Even if one cannot agree with its general conclusions about moral reasoning, it must be accepted as one of the admirable pieces of work in recent moral philosophy. It succeeds in the rare thing of expressing the reality of moral passion, than which nothing is more important to morality. As for the derived response to political violence, surely one cannot but want to share its conviction. The force of affirmation, one may think, is not made the less by matters not brought into clear consistency and order. It may be, nonetheless, that there are pressing questions which are neither answered nor excluded by what is said, but in fact raised by what is said. It may be, that is, that they are questions which have one source in nothing other than moral passion.

(Can it be, perhaps, that these questions should not be asked? Can there be a proper refusal to consider questions which presuppose that atrocities may have a defence? The idea that this is so, or that something like this is so, may be taken to play a small part in the given response to violence. It does seem true enough that there are circumstances in which we rightly say that it is right not to consider certain questions. There is little doubt, however, that these are circumstances which can be described in a more explicit and enlightening way. They are such that we already know or believe the answers to certain questions, or already know or believe enough of the answers. They are circumstances in which it is right not to *consider further*. That is, we have in fact considered the questions, or done something like it. It does not seem to me that with violence we are in the requisite position of knowledge or belief. My reasons will become apparent.)

The given response to violence is of course not to be taken just as declamation that violence is terribly wrong, but rather as an argument. Moreover, its force as declamation really must be distinguished from its force as argument. As argument, it comes to this in the main: *there is an attempt made to reason about moral issues in a certain way, but this attempt fails, and in so doing has terrible results, such as a tolerance of political violence, which tolerance is in fact ruled out by an alternative way of proceeding, which is to rely on moral necessities.*

We have here another promise, a second one, of an effective argument against violence. Let us begin at the end. It is allowed, as indeed it must be allowed, that moral necessities do sometimes conflict. It is allowed that they conflict, however, only in abnormal, painful and improbable situations. What these situations are, of course, and whether they are so rare, will be determined in part by one's conception of the extent of the moral necessities. Hampshire's conception is such that necessities having to do with distributive justice are somehow included, and the inclusion may seem undeniably right. He mentions too the necessities of helping the poverty-stricken and the destitute.

It might be taken as intended, in such responses to violence as the one we are considering, that the moral necessities having to do with not-killing are the chief moral necessities, but, more than that, they are such as to overwhelm all others. Here there is no conflict, or only a conflict quickly ended by victory. Can we take up this simple view, that there can be *no situations whatever* in which killing of whatever kind is allowed? If so, we can of course put a limit without further reflection to situations in which there can be conflict between moral necessities. The simple view may be appealing, partly for its very simplicity. If we reflect for even a moment, nonetheless, we are unlikely to be able to take it up.[12]

Those who suppose themselves to be entertaining it are almost certain not to be entertaining precisely the view that killing is not to be done no matter what numbers of deaths ensue, no matter what suffering, no matter what injustice. They are in fact likely to be thinking that we must never kill except in certain permissible situations, perhaps in the necessary extremes of self-defence, and in certain wars, and in certain instances when the state and society judge that execution is necessary, and in circumstances when an enslaved people try to throw off tyranny. Is it not impossible, however, to draw a line of this kind between the permissible area and the wholly impermissible? The reason, generally speaking, is that it must be at least a possibility that the features which make killing permissible in the one given area, certain features of injustice and suffering and so on, have counterparts in the remaining area. To put the point in the other way, there can hardly be an overwhelming moral necessity to avoid killing in the one area if there is no such thing in the other. There is not a sufficient factual difference between, say, certain tyrannies and all related situations whatever not involving tyranny, or certain 'just wars' and all related situations not involving such wars.

What we must allow is that sometimes, perhaps rarely, there is conflict between the moral necessities, including conflict involving necessities having to do with not killing. Let us for the moment suppose no more than this, that there are *some* situations, perhaps very few, in which such necessities conflict. We may have in mind a conflict between an act of killing and a course of action which will make for the persistence of some appalling misery or injustice. The question arises of what is to be done in such a situation.

We cannot do nothing. I do not mean that it would be wrong to do nothing, that doing nothing is *not morally possible*, but rather that it is not *a possibility at all* to avoid going against one moral necessity. It is not as if we can do *A*, thereby going against one moral necessity, or do *B*, thereby going against a different moral necessity, *or* do *C*, thereby going against no moral necessity. The position is that we can do only *A* or *B*, each one going against a moral necessity. It is *only* if this is the position that we in fact have a situation where there is conflict between moral necessities. To take an analogy from war, there is *no* conflict in the relevant sense between the need to save the civilians and the need for the army to advance if there is a way of doing both. To return to our own case there is no conflict between the necessity (*A*) not to kill and the necessity of (*B*) ending the misery or injustice if in fact we can do (*C*) something which respects both necessities.

If there is no possibility of an easy way, since one moral necessity or another must be denied, can we resort to something like an unreflective leap? Can we 'act spontaneously'? In most situations, although not all, this is unthinkable. There is therefore the inevitable conclusion that in almost all situations where moral necessities conflict, we must try in a rational way to do the best thing. This is not to be avoided.

What hopes can we have? An answer is that we can try to judge between alternatives, each one including the denial of a necessity. We can try to compare the two alternatives directly, or by relating both to other circumstances of which we can conceive. Would one of the two be about as bad as a third circumstance, and the other worse? (To entertain the answer that we can try to judge between alternatives, certainly, is to grant what already is sadly clear, that there is a sense of the word 'necessary' such that what we have been calling the moral necessities are not necessary. Simply to allow that there can be conflict between moral necessities is to move a good way in this direction.) The answer that we can try to compare alternatives, however, may seem to run directly against the earlier part of the given response to violence. Is comparing not just that method of moral reasoning which is said to be condemned to failure, and nevertheless to produce terrible results?

Let me try to make a bit clearer what I mean by judging between alternatives. In many forms it is not uncommon, although we overlook some instances and are not inclined to draw attention to others. Governments and also lesser officers of state weigh up possible situations such that one situation would include the taking or the loss of life, as well as a certain gain, and the other situation would involve distress or a loss, but no loss of life. This takes place in the ordinary allocation of social expenditure, notably in connection with the level of medical services. This kind of judgement has other sorts of instances. It is a part of the daily life of ordinary individuals to choose for themselves between two situations only one of which carries some risk of loss of life. It is a part of war. To return to governments, it is at the foundation of whole national policies and the conduct of international relations.

Very generally described, the procedure of judging between alternatives is one of weighing up (i) the *extent* to which and (ii) the *way* in which each of two or more alternatives would probably or certainly satisfy wants or, as we are often inclined to say, needs. Would more needs or wants be satisfied in one situation? Whose needs or wants? Would the persons benefited be those who have already been more benefited than others? This is not the procedure of judging morally which of two extents and ways of satisfaction is right, but rather the procedure of assessing extents and ways. It *is* likely to involve judgements of probability. How probable is it that certain extents and ways of satisfaction would follow from certain actions or policies? We shall look at this greatly important thing later.

This comparison is unquestionably something that in some areas and circumstances can be done well, rather than something that cannot be done at all or hardly at all. It can be done with rational confidence, very roughly speaking, when the complexity of the task is within certain bounds. It can more likely be done with such confidence, for example, when the wants or needs that would be satisfied by two possible courses of action are more or less of the same kind rather than of different kinds, or of fewer rather than more kinds. There evidently is less complication in comparing possible satisfactions of the need for food, say, than satisfactions of the needs for food on the one hand and for freedom on the other. The complexity of the task of comparison is more likely within bounds, secondly, if there are relatively simple principles as to the class or classes of people to be taken into account. It is one thing if the aim is to satisfy certain wants for as many people as possible, or indeed all persons in a society. It is another if one takes into account different classes, perhaps differentiated by the extent to which each class has already had satisfaction of wants other than those now in question, and if one then sets out to devise a policy which satisfies the wants now in question to different degrees for the different classes. The complexity of the task of comparison increases, thirdly, to the extent that wants, needs and satisfactions are interdependent. It is often true that the satisfaction of one want stands in the way of the satisfaction of another, and so on.

The idea that judgement between alternatives is impossible, that it cannot be done at all, seems to derive from confusing it with other things, including some things suggested by the given response to violence. This comparison is not a procedure whereby situations are looked at in terms of some single experienced stuff best called *the feeling of satisfaction* or indeed happiness. It is supposed, with whatever truth, that this was the recommendation of the early Utilitarians, and clearly it is true that very few of the relevant possible situations can be compared in just this way, this way alone. Indeed, many have no such ingredient. Nor can we deal in no more than a few such ingredients. This is not to say that situations cannot be weighed up in terms of the extent to which they satisfy needs and the way in which they do this. It is to be granted, too, that various things which can be called *calculation* or *computation* are impossible. Again, they are not the given comparison. It is to be granted, also, that there are difficulties, some of them notorious, in the way of systematizing or formalizing this comparison, and hence that there are no systems of a certain kind. This does not put comparison in question, or put its rationality in question.[13]

If judging between alternatives is not a method of proceeding which is always condemned to failure, it is not a method either that has an *innate* or *general* tendency to issue in terrible results. Like many other human practices, its upshots are mixed. Finally, is there any reason for thinking that comparison cannot take into account moral necessities? We have assumed that it can, and there is no reason to think otherwise, since to speak of necessities is to speak of needs, often deep needs. Not to regard them in this way would be to reduce them to mysteries.

What remains to be said, for the moment, is that it may be mistaken to think that the conflicts between moral necessities are rare or few, that the need to judge between alternatives does not arise at all often. It may be mistaken to think, more precisely, that violence rarely produces such a conflict. If that were so, it would be reasonable to say that the doctrine of moral necessities offers us an effective argument against violence, or something close to that. On the contrary, there may be many circumstances where moral necessities conflict, where moral passion divides, and such that a choice must be made between necessities. The deepest of moral feelings may not be able to save us from many large and dark questions. On the contrary, such feelings may contribute to and indeed give rise to such questions. Evidently the only possibility, if we cannot rely on a doctrine of moral necessities, is the business of judging between alternatives. We shall return to it, and to the question of how confident it can be in such an area as political violence.

It may be, then, that neither a commitment to moral necessities nor any proposition about political obligation will allow us to settle the question of violence with despatch. More generally, and still tentatively, there is the idea that there may be nothing by way of *doctrine* or *commitment* which enables us to do so. It may be that we cannot settle our minds by way of Marx's theory of history and his propositions about terrorism and revolution, or by way of lawyer-like reflections on what is sometimes called the rule of law, or by an embracing of liberal values, or by a politician's reliance on the values of negotiation and compromise, or by any version of the idea, so refuted by the course of history, or just by its wars, that those in authority know best. No more needs to be said in explanation of *doctrines and commitments* than this: they are all the supposed means but one of settling the question of violence. That remaining one is judgement between alternatives.

3. Inequalities

It will come as no great surprise that I think all doctrines and commitments *are* too weak to enable us to settle the question of violence in an effective way. There *are* facts which overwhelm any arguments about political obligation, and any residue of them. There are facts which stand in the way of our thinking that violence only rarely raises conflicts between moral necessities. It is possible to disagree, and I am aware that many people, perhaps a majority, are bound to be uncertain. There is only one way, in my view, of coming to a proper view. It is by having an immediate awareness of certain orders of fact, and by adequately reflecting on them. The first of these orders has to do with average lengths of life. The second has to do with what can be called economic and social facts. The third has to do with political inequalities. Attention was given to average lifetimes near the beginning of this book, and more is as good as essential now. Let us give it. Let us also attend a bit to the other two orders of fact. It is only through doing so that reflection about violence comes into touch with reality.

(1) Truths about average lengths of life in Britain, the United States and so on are summed up in a certain general proposition. It is that the worst-off tenths of population in terms of income, roughly speaking, in the economically developed societies, live about five years less long on average than the best-off tenths.[14] The proposition, of course, is a summary of various facts of death. In the worst-off tenths there are more infant deaths, more deaths of children, more of young people and adults due to sickness, more deaths at work and because of work, and, to a small extent, more old-age but nonetheless premature deaths.

The average life-expectancy in the economically less developed societies is about forty-two, as against seventy-one in the developed societies.[15] The difference in average life-expectancy between the worst-off tenth in the less-developed societies and the best-off tenth in the developed societies is *like a species-difference,* in the neighbourhood of forty years. Again these are summaries of various facts of death, still more grim. Again they are facts about individuals. They have precisely as much to do with individuals who have proper names as have bullets. The resulting losses of living time, to speak of them alone, are of the magnitude of many millions of years. These losses could have been prevented, and it is in fact within our power to change the future.

Shall we, as many people will want to do, give little attention to these propositions about length of life? There are particular inclinations which lead in that direction, and also several reasons, of whatever strength. I shall mention six.

There is the inclination to turn away from the subject because of the anticipation that moral or political consequences may be drawn from it. One may foresee its being argued that those who are now living shorter lives should be compensated, and that steps should be taken to change the probability that future members of the same economic classes will live shorter lives. One may foresee, too, that this argument may issue in a proposition about acts of violence directed towards compensation or change. Anticipations of this kind, while natural enough, do not give anything like a decent reason for ignoring the facts and suppositions about length of life. We need not further discuss, either, a second reluctance. It has its beginning not in the anticipation of political argument but in more unreflective feelings having to do with one's place and privilege in society, or the place and privilege of those with whom one identifies. We must resist, thirdly, that simple disinclination to consider things which may be connected in an immediate way with what every sane person regards as the horror of violence. One reason for paying attention to the darkness of our societies is that doing so may be the only tolerable way, or even the only effective way, of moving towards an ending of violence and its horror. Nor, fourthly, are the facts and suppositions about lifetimes to be put aside, because they necessarily are the beginning of an irrational appeal. By their nature they may give rise to feeling, but rationality and feeling very often come together. Indeed in certain inquiries, including our own, to inhibit feeling in certain ways is the most absurd of irrationalities.

Are the figures given in the facts and propositions to be rejected as inaccurate? The answer is that they are as accurate as a reasonable judgement requires. A careful account of them would call for many qualifications. For example, life-expectancy figures for a group at a given time are based on records of deaths in an immediately prior period. As such, they are never perfectly accurate predictions. Usually, but certainly not always, the situation will turn out to be *very slightly* better than predicted. Again, by way of random example, there is some degree of error in the calculation of the size of the fifth social class in England and Wales. The calculation is based on the reported occupations of individuals after their deaths and some misreportings occur. Such deficiencies in the figures, and others like them, do not begin to make our use of them improper.

Finally, are the facts and suppositions about lifetimes to be passed by because they are open to misconception? They *are* open to misconception, but they are none the worse for that. If we put aside everything about which mistakes can be made, we put aside everything. It would be a confusion, for example, to conceive what has been said as being about 'killings' or 'intended deaths'. It may be a mistake to say, even, that what we are considering are 'condoned shortenings of life'. Nor do our facts and suppositions concern 'violence' being done to the people who die early. As already noted, there is a persistent inclination in a part of the Left to describe almost any dark social or economic fact as a fact of violence. It is not one of my inclinations, and no such suggestion is meant. What we have before us are shortenings of life that are in a way natural and expected. That is not a reason for not attending to them, for not reflecting on them.

Let us do so, at least a little.

People now alive will live less long on average than other people in their societies, and so they will have less of what we can call the satisfaction of life, although that thin phrase does not begin to catch the reality. There are few circumstances, even near the end of one's life, where death is preferable to life, inexistence preferable to continued existence. Whatever one may think of unnaturally prolonged life, it is evident enough that an immense majority of people in the groups in question lack something which virtually everyone desires deeply and which others do possess. The fact is independent of whether or not the individuals in question ever have a thought of the likely length of their lives. Suppose that some do not. Unequal experience does not become otherwise if those who have it are unaware of the fact.

Certainly the inequality in question is an unusual one. A man who dies, although he does not enjoy a longer life, does not miss it either. He does not feel deprived or suffer a lack. It may be that this must be regarded as of importance with respect to our response to the inequality. I shall not pursue the matter except to remark that the same question must arise in other contexts. A man who dies a death by violence is not distressed thereafter either. He too does not miss what he does not have. It is always or never important that a person whose life is shortened has a lifetime unequal to the lifetimes of others. The bare fact of inequality is always or never important.

There is also the fact that some individuals are in ways aware that their lives will be shorter. There is then the matter of the felt distress that goes with the realization. No doubt it is true that non-whites in America and unskilled men in Britain, and the lowest economic tenth generally, are not troubled throughout most of their lives by the prospect that their lives will be shorter than those of others. (One can say the same, of course, of those who die deaths of violence.) There are times, nonetheless, more common in the experience of those who will die natural but earlier deaths, when there is an awareness of the prospect of a shortened life. It may be suggested, by someone resolute enough, that their feeling is unreasonable. This is so, it may be said, because they are desiring what is not possible, anguished because they will not have what in fact cannot be given to them. Let us grant, for the purpose of argument, that it is not possible *now* to change their life-expectancy. While it may have been possible in the past to do something that would have issued in a different state of affairs in the present, it is not possible now. If this makes their desire 'unreasonable', it remains a truth that they have it, and suffer because of its frustrations. A man who has been incurably blinded, who wants to see, may not cease to have his 'unreasonable' desire or his anguish. He may also have a related and absolutely reasonable desire, a desire for compensation. So with the worst-off tenth. What we have before us also touches on the desire of almost every person that certain others should live longer. The fact of a shortened life is a fact for those who live on. A part, one of many, of that experience is the experience of a mother whose children die. It is an experience of death and hence not relevant to us, but also of death before time.

Some may be stern enough to say that these last two considerations, about the conscious distress of some individuals because of their shorter lives, and the distress of those related to them, must be qualified in a certain way. Non-whites in America do not *expect* to live as long as whites. Unskilled men do not *expect* to live as long as professional men. The families of these people do not *expect* them to live so long. As a consequence, whites or professional men would be more distressed if they shared the same lesser prospect of life. That is very likely a truth. Feelings and attitudes are in part the result of anticipations. Still, the truth does not very much diminish the facts we have before us. It does not begin to give us a reason for passing quickly over the facts before us.

(2) The second order of facts may need less attention. It has to do with wealth and income, but more precisely with their consequences. To glance first at economically developed societies, it is becoming better known that the one tenth of British families, roughly speaking, that is best off in terms of wealth, has about 80 per cent of the society's total personal wealth. (The top one hundredth of British families has about 35 per cent of the total personal wealth.) The poorest tenth of families has what is sometimes called a statistically irrelevant share. They have what can best be described as none. To turn to income, which matters less, the best-off tenth receives about 23 per cent of the total income after tax. The worst-off tenth receives about 3 per cent.[16] In America there is a similarly great although a lesser inequality of wealth. The one tenth of American families who have most wealth have in fact got about 60 per cent of the total. As for the poorest tenth, it is certainly unlikely that it has as much as 1 per cent of the total personal wealth.[17] (The top one hundredth of families has about 25 per cent of the total.) The best-off tenth of American families, in terms of income, receive about 27 per cent of the total income tax. The tenth of American families that receive least in fact receive about 1 per cent of the total. The figures do not reveal that some families have quite extraordinary incomes and others have virtually no incomes at all.

Will there be greatly less inequality in the sharing of wealth twenty years from now in Britain and America? Consider the record of the past. According to a summary of calculations,[18] the best-off tenth of British families has had these percentages of the total personal wealth over about half a century:

1913	92 per cent
1930	91 per cent
1938	88 per cent
1954	79 per cent
1960	83 per cent

It is doubtful that there has been any significant improvement in the relative situation of the worst-off tenth of families during this period. As for America, there seems to have been some lessening of inequality of wealth for a few decades before about 1950. According to one calculation, however, the share of the best-off tenth of families increased from 58 per cent to 61 per cent between 1953 and 1962.[19] The worst-off tenth has perhaps improved its lot in the past half-century. Its share of wealth, of course, has not increased by so much as 1 per cent of the total.

To repeat, the best-off tenths of British and American families now have something like 80 per cent and 60 per cent of the total personal wealths of the two societies. Given the rate of change in the past, one can make a reasonable guess at what will be the state of affairs in a generation. It is that if there is no fundamental change in the two societies, the best-off tenths will have 75 per cent and 55 per cent and the poorest tenths will each have 1 per cent. In terms of income, the best-off tenths have roughly a quarter of it and the worst-off tenths something like 1/40 of it. There is unlikely to be any dramatic change for the next generation.[20] As with Britain and America, so with other economically developed Western societies. There are similar truths about present distributions of wealth and income. We can be confident, too, to turn to the next generations, that the general picture is unlikely to be greatly different.

These facts of wealth and income are not important for themselves. They are important because they are determinants and indicators of inequalities in a great part of the things that people value and need. They are determinants and indicators, more precisely, of inequalities with respect to things people will give much or indeed almost anything to have or not to have. Some few of these are shelter, security in one's place of living, privacy, a home, land; nourishment, food, delicacies; despondency about one's children, hopes and gifts for one's children; health, medical treatment with dignity, lassitude, vigour; living on welfare money, work, a career; servitude, anonymity, personal standing, rank; bitterness, envy, self-disdain, pride, feelings-in-life generally; kinds of culture, awarenesses, a sense of not being ignorant; ways of ageing and dying.

... if you're one of us, it's very bad, the water situation is. You spend a lot of your time worrying about water. That's the truth. You just don't begin a day without deciding who's going to get the water, and when, and how good it'll be when it comes back. That's why I use Coke for my children, right from the start I do. It's the best thing you can get to take away their thirst, and give them the sugar they need. They drink it all over the country, it's made for the rest of the people. If they use it, we can. We *have* to, though. We can't turn to much of anything else. There's the milk you have in your body to start out with, and that goes real fast – I hear say because we can't get enough for ourselves. My grandma, she used to say that nothing comes free, even a mother's milk, and that you plain run dry if you can't keep yourself fed up good. The one thing you *can* do is keep plenty of water inside, and that's what Cokes do, and as I say, they give you your sugar. And when the babies get on their own, they drink those Cokes and you can see them perk up, perk right up. They'll be lying around, tired-like, and waiting on me to figure out what I can find for them, and then I'll get the bottle opener and they know what's coming. My grandma, she said we'd be all dried up and dead and gone from starvation if God didn't send us Cokes.[21]

These differences between classes within the economically developed societies are but one part of the present subject, the smaller part. There are also the yet more terrible differences between the economically developed and the economically less-developed societies.

The per capita gross national product of a large number of countries in recent years was $200 *or less.*[22] This is in fact a standard definition of a less-developed country: per capita gross national product of $200 or less. The figure for many developed countries was over $1,000, with the United States being over $2,300. The average figure for the less-developed countries is of course much less than $200. These figures, of course, do not give one any direct grasp of actual incomes within the two groups of countries. They would do so if each gross national product issued in an equal income for each member of a society. The bottom tenth of population in the less-developed societies has an average income some *thousands* of times smaller than the income of the top tenth of population in developed societies. This comparison does not pertain only to small groups of people. The number of people in the bottom tenth of less-developed societies is about 200 million.

It has been a generally accepted fact that since 1965, and indeed since before then, economic inequalities between these two parts of the world have been increasing rather than decreasing. The poor countries have of course made some advances in absolute terms. Comparatively speaking, however, the poor countries have been getting poorer and the rich countries richer. Their rates of growth are such that the gap has been widening. The only thing that could reverse the trend is what amounts to an absolute transformation in the economic relations of the poor and rich countries. If it does not occur, economic inequalities between the two groups of countries, and between classes within them, will be much greater in twenty years.

It is again the consequences of these economic facts which are important. These consequences, other than those having to do with lengths of lifetimes, constitute those ways of existence which come to the attention of most of us by way of the newspaper advertisements of such admirable and in the end ineffectual organizations of international charity as Oxfam, War on Want and the Save the Children Fund. These are such consequences as the awfulnesses and horrors of starvation, lifetime hunger, disease, ignorance, begging, near-slavery, degradation. I have maintained that we must know of these things. Still, it seems that to say so little of them as could be said here in a page or two would go against a certain decency. For that reason or some other one, I shall not offer a brisk list of the facts of trachoma, or of leprosy. Nor shall I attempt to quicken anyone's appreciation of being without hope. Each of us has a clear obligation to inform himself or herself, and to come to have the feelings required not by this or that moral or political or economic outlook, but by what can be called humanity.

(3) The history of men, looked at in one direct way, has been a struggle for liberty of groups, most importantly those groups which are best described as peoples and nations. That is, it has been a struggle in which groups have sought to achieve something like an equality of autonomy with other groups. This autonomy of a people consists, roughly, in the independent governance of a homeland. It is governance by the group as distinct from some minority of it, and it is also governance free from external oppression or constraint. I take both criteria in a general way, such that England, Scotland and Wales on the one hand, and the Soviet Union on the other hand, may be said to satisfy them, although not without argument.

It is remarkably easy, if one has always been a member of a group that attained autonomy long ago, to think that groups who have not, and who struggle for autonomy, are in fact pursuing something other than a great or even a worthwhile end. They are still said to be moved by 'nationalism', a feeling or demand of an outmoded kind, not in accord with a higher ideal of human community that is now embraced, or they are taken to be engaged in a kind of meanness or selfishness peculiar to themselves. It is also remarkably easy, if one has always been a member of an autonomous group, to count the worth of autonomy for little as against the worth of something else, say some level of material well-being, or peace, or 'participation' in the governance of a homeland.

There is a clear unreality about both these thoughts. How can it be that an ideal of community or of generous humanity should lead to the idea that it is the groups having *less* or *no* autonomy which should be the first to give up what they have, or the hope of some? As for the worth of autonomy, there is a kind of absurdity in attempting to devalue it. Something for which sane and admirable men have always been willing to risk and to accept death, torture, punishment, and also self-accusation and the experience of guilt, is something worth having if anything is. There is no alternative to this conclusion.

To say these things, inevitably, is again to raise large problems.

What 'groups' count? What is a 'homeland'? I am inclined to the proposition that the most relevant answers, those to be heard first, are those given by those people who are the weaker and who define themselves as a group, an autonomy-demanding group. Their definition of themselves is most relevant, and their claim that something is their homeland is to be heard first. There is a proper presumption that they are right. No doubt it has happened that definitions and claims of this kind have sometimes been mistaken, in a large sense of the word. Perhaps this has been rare.

So much, and of course not enough, for inequalities of the third kind.

4. The principal questions

I take it now to be *established*, as the first of four conclusions of this essay, that these large and dark facts are such that *no doctrine or commitment can give us an effective argument against violence of the Left.* No doctrine or commitment enables us to settle the question. Large facts stand in the way of any progress by way of the Contract Argument for political obligation, and any progress by way of the doctrine of moral necessities. It is impossible to believe that there can be only very few relevant conflicts between moral necessities, conflicts involving the given violence. On the contrary, there can be many. In these conflicts, as in the case of reflection on the Contract Argument, we are led to judgement between alternatives. Let us return to that inevitable subject, about which the essential thing remains to be said. We can begin by recalling ends of violence of the Left, and the violence itself, and by considering the relation between these two things.

Violence can be directed to undeniably good ends. Indeed, that is an understatement. It can be directed to the changing of circumstances which are such, to describe them in one true way, that there will be a *general* agreement in the future that they were circumstances of moral barbarity. Violence can be directed, to speak differently, to ends which make for progress towards well-being for all people. As already remarked, all that I have to say concerns this violence of the Left. It is a certainty that in order to consider it one must also take account of political violence of the Right, and perhaps violence of an apolitical kind, but neither of these latter things raises the same kind of moral difficulty. There is a want of seriousness in a refusal to distinguish, say, between violence with the aim of securing a fair distribution of food, and violence with the aim of defending the special privilege of an élite, class, people or race.

It hardly needs adding that not all of the interim goals of violence of the Left are on a level. That is, some advances are of greater value, either for themselves or as means. No doubt it is generally true that the alleviation of the situation of the very worst off is the first priority. Those who are slowly starving to death have needs even greater than those who are seeking autonomy, or are defending only their liberties.

Sometimes, as with a struggle for autonomy, the end of a campaign of violence is specific enough. There has been something like exactness about the end of the Irish Republican Army or that of the black terrorists in South Africa or that of the Palestinians. In other cases, the end in view has been less specific or indeed not specific. To the extent that a specific end is insufficiently defined in a public way, or to the extent that in fact there is no specific end but only a general one, there is likely to be less chance of achieving the specific end or something of an intended sort, perhaps something within an intended range. Political violence is an attempt to coerce peoples and governments in a certain way, which is to say that it attempts to bring them to have certain attitudes and to make certain decisions. It is distinct from an exercise of force which leaves no place for decision.[23] It follows that governments and peoples must have more or less unavoidable knowledge of what is being demanded of them. One way in which a campaign of violence may fail, then, is through insufficient definition: this would be true, perhaps, of any campaign which had as its announced end anything so general as what I have given as the goal to which Left violence tends, well-being for all.

So much for ends. The second matter is violence itself. It is a mistake to avoid its true description, description which keeps its true nature in mind. The means of violence consists, in part, of atrocity and carnage. Its reality for us, in Europe at this time, is more or less immediate. That it is immediate, while the related facts of injustice are in several senses distant, is reason enough for not dwelling further on violence. This is not one-sidedness. The principal proposition is that violence gives rise to death, suffering and distress. It gives rise not merely to *probable* but to *more or less certain* death, suffering and distress.

Thirdly and most importantly, there is the resulting large matter of the relation of the means of violence to its ends, the matter of the relation of any campaign of violence to its specific or general purpose. This has to do with probabilities, and with the required sort of judgement between alternatives. Let us approach it by noticing five possible upshots of violence. Perhaps these are not quite all the relevant possibilities, and it will be apparent that they could be replaced by somewhat different classifications. This will not affect my argument.

Individuals decide on a campaign of violence directed to a specific and well-defined end, the changing or ending of an appalling circumstance, one whose persistence will cause suffering to many victims. These victims of this circumstance will live badly and perhaps briefly if the circumstance is not changed. This decision in favour of violence is of course the result, in part, of a conviction that non-violent means, or means that are less violent, will not succeed in ending or alleviating the circumstance of injustice. The campaign is taken forward, and it is resisted by the relevant government or governments, for whatever reason. It is resisted, to speak more plainly, by individuals in power, perhaps democratically elected individuals. Their resistance is successful, and so there persists the appalling circumstance to which the violence was directed. The upshot of the violence, then, is useless distress and death. This is the first of our five possible upshots of violence.

Whether the campaign of violence was right or wrong, clearly, was a matter of judgement between alternatives. In one essential part, this was the question of how probable it was in the beginning, and later, *to a reasonable judgement*, that the outcome would be what it was. Also, if a knowing judge would have found it difficult to estimate the probability of the outcome, then there necessarily was uncertainty as to whether the right course of action, whatever it was, would in fact *turn out for the best.* I take it, certainly, that kinds and degrees of ignorance or uncertainty about the results of possible actions do not make it impossible to tell which of two is right. Almost always there is a discoverable right action, an answer to the question of what ought to be done.[24] The answer is determined in part by the available knowledge, however small that knowledge. Of course, whether the right action will turn out for the best is another question. One may be less than confident about that. I shall return to this fundamental matter, and also, incidentally, to the question of the morality of the governmental resistance to violence.

To turn now to a second possibility, the violence in question is like the first in terms of the circumstance to which it is directed and the conviction that alternative non-violent means would not change the circumstance. The total result is worse. The circumstance of injustice is not changed, and, because of violence of the Right, perhaps a military take-over, there is yet more distress and death than would have been required by the government simply to defeat the campaign of violence. The upshot, then, is useless distress and death, more than in the first case. A third kind of violence is such that the end is achieved, but by means which cannot be justified by that end. That is, the total result is worse than it might have been, perhaps for the reason that the given end would have been achieved by non-violent means, which in fact were operating, or for the reason that the given end would have been achieved by non-violent means which would have been operating if there had been no violence. Again the upshot includes useless distress. The fact is not of importance, but I think there has been relatively little violence of this sort, where a circumstance of injustice or misery is in fact ended, but the means of violence were unnecessary or excessive. What is in question, of course, are not *governmental* purges, oppressions or terror campaigns. It is such things that are likely to be *excessive* as means to an achieved end, of whatever morality.

A fourth possibility is that violence achieves its end, the end being worth it. A circumstance of great injustice is ended within a given time, and the terrible cost was nonetheless not too great. Non-violence would not have worked. Many of the revolutions and struggles of the past which now are celebrated as beginnings of national histories are taken to be in this category. Again, of course, the question of the rightness of the actions in question is to be settled, in an essential part, by what the probability was of achieving the given end. A fifth possible situation is one where the violence does not achieve its specific end, but does issue in a related state of affairs, or where violence has a general rather than a specific end, and does achieve something of the envisaged general kind. Non-violence would not have worked. The total result is better than the alternative. Certainly there has been violence of this fifth kind. I doubt that there is any serious outlook, short of an absolute passivism, which in the late twentieth century can perhaps no longer be serious, that does not have the consequence that there have been many cases of the fifth kind, and of course the fourth.

The essential and principal issue, of course, is whether anyone can say with rational confidence, at or near the beginning, that some envisaged violence will have one of the five possible upshots rather than others. What is needed is an answer to that question. More generally, what is needed is an answer to a question, or indeed many questions, of this general form:

> Which is right, *non-violent action* at a cost of distress D_1 and with a probability P_1 of ending or altering a circumstance M_1 of misery or injustice within the time T_1, or *violence* at a cost of distress D_2 and with a probability P_2 of ending or altering a circumstance M_2 of misery or injustice within the time T_2?

To answer a question of this form is of course to do what was called judging between alternatives.

Suppose, for a moment, that in a given circumstance we can replace D_1 with a specific description of the costs of distress, if any, of non-violence. It may be, of course, that the relevant distress of non-violent activity comes to nothing. We can also give a specific value to D_2, which will certainly be harder. That is, we can say with some assurance what the distress of the contemplated violence would be. Finally, we have a grasp of M_1, which may or may not be the same as M_2, and of T_1 and T_2, which may or may not be identical. *Can* there be confidence in giving values to P_1 and P_2? *Can* we say with confidence what probability there is of the non-violence being successful, and what probability there is of the violence being successful?

Given each of D_1 and D_2, and M_1 and M_2, and T_1 and T_2, it may be taken that if P_1 is below a certain level, and if P_2 is above a certain level, then an answer to the question can be had with confidence. That is, if the probability of non-violence being successful is below a certain level, and the probability of violence being successful is above a certain level, then an answer that violence is the right course can be made with confidence. On the other hand, if P_1 is above the critical level or if P_2 is below the other critical level, then another answer can be had with confidence. That is, if the likelihood of non-violence being a success is above the critical level, and the likelihood of violence being a success is below the other critical level, then the answer that violence is wrong can be made with confidence.

In the nature of things, however, P_1 will usually be *near its critical level* and P_2 *near its critical level*. This guarantees difficulty, at least difficulty. In the nature of things, to speak differently, it will be unlikely that a government and society are such as to make it relatively highly probable (well above a critical level) that they will give in to non-violence, while it is of relatively low probability (well below the critical level) that they will give in to violence. The general reason for this is a certain rationality. To express it simply, if the opponents of a government have a 75 per cent chance of winning by resort to violence, then it will be reasonable for the government to bargain or compromise. There will be, that is, a decent probability of the opponents of the government achieving their goal non-violently. It is unlikely to happen that the opponents of the government have a 75 per cent chance of winning by violence while there is a relatively low probability of their winning by non-violence. It is unlikely, indeed, that the opponents have a 50 per cent chance of winning by violence while there is a relatively low probability of their winning by non-violence. On the other hand, if the opponents have only a 5 per cent chance of winning by violence, then there will be less incentive for the government to bargain. There will be little probability of the opponents getting their way by non-violence. It will be a rare case where the opponents have so small a chance of getting their way by violence and a relatively large probability of getting it non-violently.

In general, then, the probabilities will be close to their critical levels. There is the consequence, a large consequence, that *a rational confidence will require fairly precise judgements of probability.* Ordinarily, rough and hence more secure judgements will not be sufficient. A rough and secure judgement of probability will leave one with no decision whatever on the critical issue. There is no use in the judgement that there is a 60 per cent or 70 per cent chance of success, if the question of whether or not to go ahead depends on whether the chance is over or under 65 per cent.

I am inclined to the unhappy view that for the most part we cannot judge the relevant probabilities with the precision needed for rational confidence. Certainly judgement between alternatives is necessary, and almost certainly there is a right judgement. That it can be made with rational confidence is unlikely.

There is an argument of another kind for this conclusion. Essentially it is that there has been a general failure to estimate such probabilities precisely in the past, and that the reasons for this are likely to persist into the future. There has not been anything like confirmation of claims to the effect that a certain proportion of campaigns of violence of a given sort will result in situations of a certain kind. No one has found identifying marks by which to decide that a conceived campaign is to a certain extent probable to have one of the first three upshots rather than the fourth or fifth. Indeed, there has not even been much success in just the *formulating* of such claims. This essential prior activity, which might also be called the devising of hypotheses, has itself turned out to be pretty well impossible. It has been impossible to produce testable claims which have some possibility of being useful.

The formulating and confirming of such claims would have been the result, of course, of study of the past. In fact, this endeavour of formulating and confirming claims could hardly have been distinct from another one, the giving of explanations of past sequences of events, past successes and failures. There is very little available by way of such explanations. If anything remotely like 'laws of history' have been discovered, they have not been such as to enable historians to offer persuasive explanations of successes and failures in past political struggles. Certainly there should now be universal agreement that speculative philosophy of history, the pursuit of 'laws of history', has been a dismal failure. If we can be confident that some past event was a *necessary* condition of a subsequent one, we cannot be anything like confident about what set of events was a *sufficient* condition for the subsequent one.

This failure to explain the outcomes of past struggles, and hence to arrive at claims for use in the present and future, has several explanations, and they are truisms. One is that so many different factors enter into the producing of successes and failures. The range of relevant factors for a violent political struggle is exceedingly wide. The outcome of a violent struggle depends on (1) *the opposition to the government*, which may be taken to vary as a function of at least its size, social base or support, principles, ideology, aims and strategy, leadership, finances, organizational competence and weapons, (2) *the government's strength*, which has to do with at least the government's form, popularity, competence, resources and stability, and (3) the *international environment*, which includes the influence and support of other governments, movements and groups, changing relationships between them, and also the influence and pressure of international opinion.[25]

A second explanation of failure in explaining and predicting violent political struggles is that there is relatively little data to go on. This will only seem surprising or paradoxical to those who forget that we cannot for purposes of experiment increase the number or kind of such struggles. In most of science, by contrast, we can so act as to produce more and more data. A third and large explanation is the nature of history: there is not enough repetition in it to enable us to learn enough from it. Changes in technology are part of this story. Changes in ideology are as important, as are changing conceptions of what is within the realm of the possible. History is the product of human invention of several kinds, and endless invention gives rise to endless change.

These explanations of past failure to explain and predict political struggles evidently suggest that the failure will persist. Particularly the third explanation, the nature of history, makes it unlikely that we shall come to do better.

For the most part, then, we cannot make adequate assessments of the probability that political action or inaction will have a certain result, that an envisaged campaign of violence will be of one of the five kinds. We cannot make assessments adequate for a rational confidence. *For the most part, for we cannot be at all confident that our judgements that a campaign of violence is wrong or right will turn out well. We cannot have the reassurance that doing the right thing, as we see it, will have the best upshot. For the most part we are subject to uncertainty.* That is the second conclusion of this essay, not much diminished by the qualification that in some cases we can judge probabilities with confidence and so come to decently based verdicts. These will include some in which violence is judged right and some in which it is judged wrong. Democratic violence comes to mind in the first connection.

Some will be inclined to agree that an extensive uncertainty is indeed unavoidable, and then pass on to this: even when violence is judged to be right, the judgement will quite possibly turn out badly, and so there is the general conclusion that violence must not be used. We cannot have the reassurance of such a proposition. There is *as much* reason to move from the given uncertainty to the proposition that even when violence is judged to be wrong, the judgement will quite possibly turn out to involve a mistake, and so we can conclude that violence *may* be used. There is, of course, a long tradition which derives kinds of reassuring conservatism from claims about our ignorance. We must not do this or that, leaving the well-tried path, because we do not know what dangers lie to one side. Whatever is to be said of all that, my claim about our uncertainty is such that it has neither a reassuring nor an unreassuring upshot. If we are uncertain in the given way, any inference to conservatism is worthless. The well-tried path is no more known to be correct than any other path.

Despite all of what has been said, this conclusion about uncertainty would have about it a certain strangeness if it were, so to speak, the whole truth. This strangeness, looked at one way, would be the strangeness of finding very little of a substantial kind in the long historical endeavour of so many people, including moral and political philosophers and theorists. To speak differently, the strangeness would derive from a conviction that while our position with respect to much violence may be one of uncertainty, it is not only that. Surely we do also have certainty of certain kinds, or anyway decently grounded belief. There is then something else to be said in connection with the general moral question of political violence of the Left. It is my third conclusion. It pertains, incidentally, to other general moral questions and not only to violence.

We have been concerned so far, essentially, with an *overriding* question. However, we can attempt to have other moral views of an action than just an overriding one. This seems always overlooked in such contexts as our present one. It is not that we can attempt only two possible views, expressed indifferently by such pairs of terms as 'right' and 'wrong', 'justified' and 'unjustified', 'correct' and 'mistaken', 'ought' and 'ought not', 'morally necessary' and 'not morally necessary'. Or rather, it is not that we can take up only one of several overriding moral views, since, to mention one other, there is also the overriding view that the fundamental question is one whose answer must be uncertain. It is also true, to come to the point, that acts can have features and effects about which we are certain, perhaps many. An act can then stand in comparisons to many other acts.

Let us say that both of two acts of bombing were wrong. It remains of obvious importance that one had a definition having to do with a struggle against injustice, and the other did not. It is probable that each act made for *some* progress or movement in the direction supported by the respective agents. This is then a way in which the first act, although it will not achieve a given end, and hence was wrong, has something to be said for it, which the second does not. The same sort of argument has a fairly wide application. Consider again the first act of bombing, and also the replying activity of the state. We may suppose that there is no killing or wounding in the latter activity, except in self-defence. We may suppose that but for the opposition of the state, the injustice in question would be ended or affected. It is possible, then, while taking both the violent act and the replying activity of the state to be wrong, to see a respect in which the act has a recommendation not had by the activity. There is also the clear respect having to do with death and injury, in which the state's activity is superior.

It seems to follow from this view of violence, as being open to more judgements than just two or three, that a certain policy with respect to certain movements should be adopted, a policy which comprehends realities. It is unlikely that it will be, except insofar as the interests of national states conflict. It is, roughly, that the treatment accorded to violent movements, some of them, should be different. By way of one illustration, it seems to be entirely arguable that the Irish Republican Army and groups around it should have the possibility of stating their claims in public forums in Britain. My third conclusion, then, is that *if we cannot with confidence make overriding judgements about violence, we can make lesser judgements, and they are of some value as guides to action.*

The last of my conclusions also has to do with comparisons, two comparisons between campaigns of violence on the one hand and, on the other, the policies and practices of the individuals who are the reality of sovereign states. We can proceed here in terms of overriding views.

Of the mentioned categories of campaigns of violence, the first three worsen situations rather than improve them, and the others do the opposite. For the most part, it is impossible to have a rational confidence at the outset that a judgement for or against will turn out well. There are, of course, also some other situations where it *is* possible to have a rational confidence or perhaps to be rationally certain. Let us have one of these in mind in connection with the first comparison. Let us suppose that there *is* rational certainty that an ongoing campaign of violence is in fact of the first kind. That is, it is directed to the ending of a circumstance of misery, but it will not succeed, because of resistance by the individuals who constitute the executive of the relevant state. If the perpetuation of the campaign of violence is wrong, there can be an argument to the conclusion that *resistance by the individuals of the state, who also bear proper names, is as wrong as the campaign of violence*. Without their resistance, the circumstance of misery would be ended. There is also another comparison. The campaign of violence is mistaken only *because of* the resistance of the government. That is, without the resistance the campaign would not be mistaken. On the other hand, it is not true that the governmental resistance is wrong *because of* the campaign of violence.

Many will want to resist something here. One inapposite line of resistance has to do with making a moral assessment of the two groups of persons or agents involved. Such an assessment is not the main thing. There are individuals who engage in violence out of *non-moral motivation*, and there are individuals who oppose them out of equally non-moral motivation, having been corrupted by power, or having become representatives of no more than the self-interest of a group, perhaps vicious self-interest. There are individuals who engage in violence, and by so doing show themselves to be of *moral motivation*, whether or not their judgements as to their actions are correct, and the same is true of some of those in power who oppose them.

The main thing is not in this way about agents, but about acts. It is about questions of this kind: taking an act in itself and for its consequences, ought it to be performed? Of course, as we know, the question can be couched in terms of conceivable agents. Characterizing the act in terms of possible motives and beliefs, we may ask if it is an act that would be performed by a certain knowing judge. As already indicated,[26] I do not have in mind what might be called an Ideal Agent, one who has greater sympathy, knowledge or whatever than can humanly be had, but something in the line of an actual person, although one with some attributes and not others.

The kind of violence-situation described is one in which the violence would be wrong, but where the governmental response would also be wrong. Without that response, or rather, with a different response which is a possibility, there would be a changing or ending of the relevant unjust circumstance, perhaps one of misery. Can this be resisted appositely? Can it be shown that there are no such cases? It seems likely that many attempts will involve recourse to a doctrine of political obligation, about which we know, or perhaps to some sort of commitment to moral necessities, of which we know something, or to some other essentially indecisive consideration. What would be decisive would be the proposition that if national states were to end a circumstance of injustice, that would in fact always result in a greater one. It seems to me that this cannot be shown.

There is also the second comparison, my main one. Suppose that the situation is the more common one where it is *not* possible to have confidence about one's judgement that the campaign of violence is right or wrong. What is also true of the situation is that the circumstance of misery might be changed or ended *by governmental action.* Individuals in government have a considerable opportunity to secure this end *without violence.* They have a considerable opportunity to end misery without thereby causing suffering. That they do not do this is wrong. *This* judgement is not like the other in being so open to the possibility of going wrong. Here we have a small asymmetry, but one which throws into sharp definition the historic and continuing practices of sovereign states, or rather the individuals at their heads. It is a settled fact, about which there can be hardly any doubt, that their obligations are great. *An increasing perception of this great obligation, and of great failure in it, will be a recommendation of much violence.* This is my fourth conclusion.

Certain propositions about political obligation, like others about moral necessities, do not enable us to settle the general moral question of political violence of the Left. Nor does any other doctrine or commitment. This is so because of certain grim facts of inequality. All that we can do is attempt to judge between alternatives. This, in large part, cannot be anything like confident. We cannot escape uncertainty about the overriding question. It is an uncertainty, however, in which certain limited perceptions and responses are possible. The most important of these may be the perception of the wrongfulness of the historic and continuing practices of sovereign states, or, more to the point, of the individuals who are the reality of those sovereign states.

I said in starting that I wished to say some things in advocacy of a certain response to the question of violence of the Left. In finishing, it is worth saying that I do take political philosophy to consist in *advocacy*. It is a kind of analogue to the adversarial system in some systems of law, including the British. Political philosophers are inevitably more like barristers, as distinct from judges, than is allowed by certain high conceptions of their subject, and it is best to admit it. No doubt they are advocates more or less convinced of the rightness of their cases, but they are advocates nonetheless.

NOTES

I On Inequality and Violence, and Differences We Make between Them

1. *Statistical Abstract of the United States: 1974* (Washington, 1975), Table 80, p. 58. Cf. 1977 edition (Washington, 1978), Table 94, p. 65.

2. In 1920 the gap between non-whites and whites was about ten years, in 1930 about thirteen years, in 1940 about eleven years, in 1950 about eight years, in 1960 about seven years and in 1970 about seven years. Op. cit., Table 80, p. 58.

3. R. Leete and A. J. Fox, 'Registrar General's Social Classes: Origins and Uses', *Population Trends*, 8 (1977), 1–7.

4. *Occupational Morality, Decennial Supplement, 1970–72* (London, 1978), p. 190.

5. See, for example, A. B. Atkinson, *Wealth, Income and Inequality* (Penguin, 1973).

6. Source: *United Nations Demographic Yearbook 1973* (New York, 1974), Table 18, p. 336. The figures in my table, like the figures in the source-table, have to do with different years. Cf. subsequent yearbooks.

7. Simon Kuznets, 'The Gap: Concept, Measurement, Trends', in *The Gap Between Rich and Poor Nations*, edited by Gustav Ranis (Macmillan, 1972), p. 34.

8. Source: *Statistical Abstract of the United States: 1974*, Table 80, p. 58.

9. Robert McNamara, *Address to the Board of Governors* of the International Bank for Reconstruction and Development (1970), p. 8.

10. Robert Coles, *Still Hungry in America* (Cleveland, 1969), pp. 27–8.

11. See below, Essay 3, Part 1, and Essay 4, Part 2. See also Jerome A. Shaffer (ed.), *Violence* (New York, 1971), which contains several essays on the definition of violence.

12. For the other, see Essay 5, Part 3.

13. I have in mind such a procedure as the one made clear by R. M. Hare, *Freedom and Reason* (Oxford University Press, 1963). For an

economical and acute account of reasonings found in the history of political theory, see Leslie J. Macfarlane, *Political Disobedience* (Macmillan, 1972). Hannah Arendt, in 'On Violence', an essay in *Crises of the Republic* (Penguin, 1973), discusses some of them enlighteningly.

14. By Leon Trotsky.

15. *Herr Eugen Dühring's Revolution in Science* (*Anti-Dühring*), trans. E. Burns (New York, 1966), p. 109.

16. Marx-Engels, *The German Ideology*, ed. R. Pascal (Lawrence & Wishart, 1939).

17. Bentham, *The Handbook of Fallacies*, p. 207. Mill, *On Liberty*, p. 70 (Everyman edition).

18. J. J. C. Smart and Bernard Williams, *Utilitarianism: For and Against* (Cambridge University Press, 1973), pp. 97–8.

19. ibid., pp. 116–17, 103–4.

20. ibid., p. 94.

21. ibid., pp. 102–3.

22. ibid., p. 103.

23. ibid., pp. 88–9.

24. Williams considers this sort of suggestion, that consequentialist attitudes may be seen as supporting the chemist's decision. His remarks, I think, do not really undercut the suggestion.

25. Essay 5, Part 2.

26. *Conjectures and Refutations: The Growth of Scientific Knowledge* (Routledge, 1963), p. 355. For a related discussion of Popper, see Roy Edgley, 'Reason and Violence', in S. Körner (ed.), *Practical Reason* (Blackwell, 1974).

27. Popper, op. cit., p. 363.

28. ibid., p. 358.

29. ibid., p. 357.

30. Stuart Hampshire discusses and defends Bertrand Russell's relevant condemnation of governments in 'Russell, Radicalism, and Reason', in *Philosophy and Political Action* (Oxford University Press, 1972), edited by Virginia Held, Kai Nielsen and Charles Parsons.

31. Essay 5, Part 4.

32. An extended attempt has been made by John Rawls in *A Theory of Justice* (Oxford University Press, 1972). A principal part of his doctrine is discussed in the third essay of this book.

33. The following recent writings, while of different kinds, qualities and sympathies, share at least the feature of overlooking what I call the Principle of Equality: S. I. Benn and R. S. Peters, *Social Principles and the Democratic State* (Allen & Unwin, 1959), Chapter 5; W. T. Blackstone, 'On the Meaning and Justification of the Equality Principle', *Ethics*, 1967; Norman E. Bowie, 'Equality and Distributive Justice', *Philosophy*, 1970; John Charvet, 'The Idea of Equality as a Substantive Principle of Society',

Political Studies, 1969; J. R. Lucas, *The Principles of Politics* (Oxford University Press, 1966), Section 56, and 'Against Equality', *Philosophy*, 1965; Felix E. Oppenheim, 'Egalitarianism as a Descriptive Concept', *American Philosophy Quarterly*, 1970; D. D. Raphael, *Problems of Political Philosophy* (Macmillan, 1970), pp. 183–94; John Rees, *Equality* (Macmillan, 1972), Chapters 7 and 8; Nicholas Rescher, *Distributive Justice* (Indianapolis, 1966), Chapter 4; Bernard Williams, 'The Idea of Equality', in Peter Laslett and W. G. Runciman (eds.), *Philosophy, Politics and Society*, Second Series (Blackwell, 1962).

2 Our Omissions and Their Violence

1. See the admirable book by Jonathan Glover, *Causing Death and Saving Lives* (Penguin, 1977), particularly Chapter 7, and an alarming short article, 'The Survival Lottery' (*Philosophy*, 1975) by John Harris.

2. The example is owed to Philippa Foot, who writes that 'most of us allow people to die of starvation in India and Africa, and there is surely something wrong with us that we do; it would be nonsense, however, to pretend that it is only in law that we make a distinction between allowing people in the underdeveloped countries to die of starvation and sending them poisoned food. There is worked into our moral system a distinction between what we owe people in the form of aid and what we owe them in the way of non-interference' ('The Problem of Abortion and the Doctrine of Double Effect', *The Oxford Review*, 1967).

3. In *Utilitarianism: For and Against* (Cambridge University Press, 1973) Bernard Williams discusses the case of a man who must choose between the act of shooting one political protester himself, or omitting to do so, with the result that someone else will shoot twenty.

4. In ordinary morality there is a distinction between what we are obliged to do, and what is done by those who are or used to be called saints and heroes. They are those individuals, such as Albert Schweitzer, who are said to be moved by an ideal, and so to do more than their duty. It is said that they do things of moral excellence, but they would not do wrong if they did not do them. They do some of the things that we omit to do.

All this is mistaken if the argument I have been supporting is correct. Those who are commended as going far beyond their duty may not be doing much more than just their duty. They are doing things such that if they did not do them, they *could* be reproached.

Ordinary morality, with the distinction just noticed, has not been without its advocates. Mr J. O. Urmson is one. He tells us ('Saints and Heroes', in A. I. Melden, ed., *Essays in Moral Philosophy*, Seattle, 1958), that 'it would be quite ridiculous for everyone, however circumstanced, to be expected to go off and nurse lepers'. Does he tell us, however, why a somewhat more sane expectation, but of the same impulse, would be wrong?

He does declare that it is the duties of ordinary morality, which of course *allow* omissions of the kind we have been considering, that are the important thing: they secure that life is not 'brutish and short'. The phrase is unfortunate. 'Brutish and short' lives, for some, are guaranteed precisely by our not going beyond duty, so-called, by our persisting in some ordinary omissions.

A second of his contentions is that duties more stringent, more in line with the argument I have been supporting, could not be kept by us. All duties, including the less stringent, would then come to lack urgency. We would come to have that supposed upshot upon which scores of Utilitarian arguments rest, and whose improbability undermines them, 'a general breakdown of compliance with the moral code'.

The other relevant contentions, in my view, are about as hopeless. The third is that a moral code must be made up of rules whose complexity is not so great as to be unmanageable; the fourth is that we cannot have a morality which involves the possibility of too much expectation and too great a demand on individuals; and the fifth, not entirely unrelated, is that free choice in moral matters, rather than the constraining weight of obligation, is better wherever tolerable.

5. This possible objection was suggested to me by Janet Richards.

3 On Two Pieces of Reasoning about Our Obligation to Obey the Law

1. Part 3.

2. Robert Paul Wolff, 'On Violence', *Journal of Philosophy*, 66 (1969), pp. 601–16; *In Defence of Anarchism* (New York, 1970). One commentary on Wolff's work is *In Defence of Political Philosophy* (New York, 1972) by Jeffrey H. Reiman.

3. John Rawls, *A Theory of Justice* (Oxford University Press, 1972). Most of the book is not unlike Rawls's earlier essays. These include 'Justice as Fairness', in *Philosophy, Politics and Society*, Second Series, ed. Peter Laslett and W. G. Runciman (Blackwell, 1962), pp. 132–57; 'Distributive Justice', in *Philosophy, Politics and Society*, Third Series, ed. Laslett and Runciman (Blackwell, 1969), pp. 58–82; 'The Justification of Civil Disobedience', in *Civil Disobedience: Theory and Practice*, ed. Hugo Adam Bedau (New York, 1969), pp. 240–55.

4. *Can* this concession be expressed even covertly as the concession that the distinctive political concept of violence is empty and that talk which uses it is incoherent? Is there no sense in talk of a use of force prohibited by a government which has a right to unreflective obedience? Well, we can *conceive* of a government which is in fact accorded a right it ought not to have. We can conceive, further, that it puts the usual pro-

hibitions on certain uses of force. There are more problems here. The substantial conclusion of the argument is preserved in the overt form given above, however, so let us stick to that. I mean the proposition that the violent cannot be condemned for failing in a certain obligation, for going against a certain authority.

5. We are told that 'claims to authority', the authority related to unreflective obedience, 'have been defended on a variety of grounds, most prominent among which are the appeal to God, to tradition, to expertise, to the laws of history, and to the consent of those commanded' ('On Violence', p. 603). Later (p. 612) it seems to be assumed that the argument of the essay has shown 'the classical theory of political authority' to be mistaken.

6. *A Theory of Justice*, p. 302.

7. op. cit., pp. 17, 21, 42, 167 and 577–87. The basic proposition is also thought to have two other uses, which I do not consider here. See my article, 'The Use of the Basic Proposition of a Theory of Justice', *Mind*, 1975.

8. op. cit., pp. 12, 120; cf. pp. 15, 18, 120, 121 and 521.

9. Rawls has in mind different things in different places. In 'The Justification of Civil Disobedience', op. cit., he appears to be dealing with actual societies.

10. See above, p. 117.

11. For a relevant discussion by Rawls, but not one which materially affects the point, see *A Theory of Justice*, pp. 577–87.

12. op. cit., pp. 14–21, 587.

13. I have left out, incidentally, some formal conditions on principles that might be taken to be part of the first premise of the Contract Argument, and also some practical considerations. Both can evidently also go into the Ordinary Argument. Op. cit., pp. 46, 175.

14. op. cit., p. 13.

15. Rawls, in passing and perhaps implicitly, grants the point. Op. cit., p. 139.

16. A second objection to my fundamental criticism would have to do with a view of the Contract Argument as other than a plain matter of premises and conclusion. See pp. 21, 48–9, 579. One can, however, take the same view of the Ordinary Argument.

17. 'Distributive Justice', op. cit., pp. 73–5.

18. Essay 5, Part 1.

4 On Democratic Violence

1. Jean-Paul Sarte, preface to Frantz Fanon, *The Wretched of the Earth*, trans. Constance Farrington (Penguin, 1970). A similar idea is at the centre of George Sorel's *Reflections on Violence*. For an enlightening account

of Sorel's thought, see Isaiah Berlin's lecture printed in *The Times Literary Supplement*, No. 3,644, 31 December 1971.

2. Herbert Marcuse, 'Ethics and Revolution', *Revolution and the Rule of Law*, ed. Edward Kent (Englewood Cliffs, N. J., 1971).

3. Essay 3, Parts 4–7.

4. Compare, for example, Robert Dahl, *A Preface to Democratic Theory* (Chicago, 1956), p. 84.

5. See, for example, the essays by Robert Audi, Robert L. Holmes and Ronald S. Miller, in *Violence*, ed. Jerome A. Shaffer (New York, 1971).

6. Marcuse, in an article in the *New York Times Magazine*, 27 October 1968, associates himself with this view. See also John Harris, 'The Marxist Conception of Violence', *Philosophy and Public Affairs*, 1974.

7. See above, Essay 3, Parts 1–3.

8. pp. 22–3.

9. Dahl, *A Preface to Democratic Theory*, p. 72.

10. As, of course, does Rawls.

11. All or most of them are given by Henry B. Mayo, *An Introduction to Democratic Theory* (New York, 1960).

12. Rawls (*A Theory of Justice*, p. 366 and elsewhere) suggests that violence cannot be a 'mode of address', a form of notice given to a society that injustice exists. If it is true that violence cannot be described as a 'mode of address', it is also true that typically it does not consist in the coercion of force. My argument depends in part on this latter point rather than any doubtful suggestion about a close connection between violence and more formal or venerable proceedings. In my view, as may be anticipated, violence may on occasion be described as 'an appeal to the sense of justice of the majority', which Rawls appears to deny.

5 Four Conclusions about Political Violence of the Left

1. Essay 2.

2. Thomas Hobbes, *Leviathan*, Chapters 26 and 30.

3. John Locke, *Second Treatise of Government*, Chapters 16–19.

4. J.-J. Rousseau, *A Discourse on Political Economy*.

5. Essay 3, Parts 4–6.

6. Cf. Peter Singer, *Democracy and Disobedience* (Oxford University Press, 1973).

7. Cf. J. L. Austin, *How To Do Things With Words* (Oxford University Press, 1962).

8. There are insuperable difficulties in trying to argue from these three considerations to the existence of an actual agreement, as distinct from a general expectation. To mention a less obvious one of these difficulties, the Agreement Argument presumably requires that the state or society make a *uniform* offer to all members of society, the same offer for each member.

What is it? Is any *uniform* thing that can be found also substantial? Certainly we can find a far from uniform pattern in the actual provision of opportunities, protections, rôles and so on to individuals by the state.

9. See R. M. Hare, 'Political Obligation', in Ted Honderich (ed.), *Social Ends and Political Means* (Routledge, 1976).

10. Cf. Singer, op. cit. See also above, Essay 3, Part 7.

11. Stuart Hampshire, *Morality and Pessimism*, the Leslie Stephen Lecture, 1972 (Cambridge University Press, 1972). Mr Hampshire has not written substantially about political violence, but I have (since writing this essay) come upon a transcript of a television talk by him. (*The New Review*, Vol. 2, No. 24, March 1967). He says in part:

'... a moral rule against all assassinations for political reasons is needed, even though there will be very unusual and extreme circumstances in which an assassination in peacetime is justified. For example, if a group of prominent Germans had arranged the assassination of Hitler in August, 1939, with a view to making peace, it is my opinion that they would have acted rightly; the prolonged horrors and the vast cruelties avoided would have outweighed the evil example in this extreme and exceptional case. Moreover, he was already a multiple murderer. But I still think, from my own moral position, that one ought to be shocked by the idea of political assassination, and that there ought to be a strongly felt rule against it, in spite of these extreme, exceptional cases. One has to have moral rules, backed by moral feeling attached to the rules, even if in very exceptional circumstances, such as the Hitler one, it may be permissible to break the rule ...

'... the straight, clear question in the title of this series ('Does a political cause ever give us the right to kill?') deserves a straight, clear answer; or at least a fairly clear one, if the issue is too complex for complete clarity: yes, a political cause does sometimes give us the right to kill: in a war for the defence of one's country, but not in an unnecessary, unjust, undeclared, useless war, as in Vietnam. I will suggest the beginnings of a rough criterion for justified killing in very extreme situations in peacetime. Four conditions are necessary: first, that it is a response to a great injustice and oppression, as of a resistance movement against a foreign power ruling by force and terror so that the victim is the reverse of innocent; secondly, that it is certain that no lawful and non-violent means of remedying the injustice and oppression will be given: thirdly, that the political killing will certainly cause far less suffering, and less widespread suffering than the present injustice and cruelty are causing: lastly, that it really is very probable that the killing will end the oppression, and that it will not provoke more violence and more horror; this last condition is very rarely satisfied, but sometimes it may have been. These principles give the outline of a possible morality of political violence, though of course a highly disputable one.'

12. Views and problems of this kind are admirably discussed by Jonathan Glover in *Causing Death and Saving Lives* (Penguin, 1977).

13. Cf. James Griffin's excellent inquiry, 'Are There Incommensurable Values?', *Philosophy and Public Affairs*, Vol. 7, No 1, Fall 1977.

14. See Essay 1, Part 1.

15. See Essay 1, Part 1.

16. See, for example, A. B. Atkinson, *Wealth, Income and Inequality* (Penguin, 1973); Atkinson and A. J. Harrison, *Distribution of Personal Wealth in Britain* (Cambridge, 1977). See also *The Times*, 2 June 1978, and the *Guardian*, 12 July 1979, for related figures.

17. Robert J. Lampman, 'Income and Inequality: the 1930s to the 1960s', in *Poverty and Affluence*, 2nd edition (New York, 1970), ed. Robert E. Will and Harold G. Vatter.

18. Atkinson, op. cit., p. 21.

19. Lampman, op. cit., p. 51.

20. In order to arrive at some guess as to the state of incomes twenty years from now, if an unprecedented change does not occur, let us again look to the past. The top tenth of British families, according to one calculation (H. F. Lydall, 'The Long-Term Trend in Size-Distribution of Income', *Royal Statistical Society Journal*, 1959, p. 14), received roughly these percentages of the total income after tax in the years in question:

1938	34 per cent
1949	27 per cent
1957	23·5 per cent

During the same period, no doubt, there was some increase in the percentage income that was received by the one tenth of British families with the worst income. Given the record, and the calculation that the top tenth now receives about 25 per cent of the total and the bottom tenth about 2 per cent or 3 per cent, it is a reasonable guess that in twenty years the top tenth of British families will receive something of the order of 15 per cent of the income and the bottom tenth something like 5 per cent.

In the United States, according to one calculation (James G. Scoville (ed.), *Perspectives on Poverty and Income Distribution*, Lexington, Mass., 1971, p. 18), the best-paid and the worst-paid fifths (not tenths) of families received these percentages of total income in the years mentioned:

1936	52 per cent	4 per cent
1947	46 per cent	5 per cent
1962	45 per cent	5 per cent

To return to our chosen categories, tenths of American families, we have it that the top tenth now has about 27 per cent of the total income and the bottom tenth about 1 per cent. The state of affairs in twenty years, if there is no radical transformation of American society, may be that the top tenth will have something like 23 per cent of the total income and the bottom tenth will have something like 3 per cent.

21. Robert Coles, *Still Hungry in America* (Cleveland, 1969) pp. 40–41.

22. Jagdish Bhagwati, *The Economics of Underdeveloped Countries* (Weidenfeld & Nicolson, 1971), p. 14.

23. See Essay 4, Part 5.

24. Essay 2, Part 6, includes more on these matters, of course.

25. Cf. Paul Wilkinson, *Terrorism and the Liberal State* (London, 1977), pp. 82–3.

26. Essay 2, Part 6.

INDEX